LAMENTATIONS

WISDOM COMMENTARY

Volume 30

Lamentations

Gina Hens-Piazza

Carol J. Dempsey, OP
Volume Editor

Barbara E. Reid, OP
General Editor

A Michael Glazier Book

LITURGICAL PRESS
Collegeville, Minnesota

www.litpress.org

A Michael Glazier Book published by Liturgical Press

1   2   3   4   5   6   7   8   9

Library of Congress Cataloging-in-Publication Data

Names: Hens-Piazza, Gina, 1948– author.
Title: Lamentations / Gina Hens-Piazza ; Carol J. Dempsey, OP, volume editor, Barbara E. Reid, OP, general editor.
Description: Collegeville, Minnesota : Liturgical Press, 2017. | Series: Wisdom commentary ; Volume 30 | "A Michael Glazier book." | Includes bibliographical references and index.
Identifiers: LCCN 2017022472 (print) | LCCN 2017000813 (ebook) | ISBN 9780814681794 (ebook) | ISBN 9780814681541 (hardcover)
Subjects: LCSH: Bible. Lamentations—Commentaries. | Catholic Church—Doctrines.
Classification: LCC BS1535.53 (print) | LCC BS1535.53 .H46 2017 (ebook) | DDC 224/.307—dc23
LC record available at https://lccn.loc.gov/2017022472

For Amy and Hannah . . .
and all my other faithful women friends on the journey

Contents

Abbreviations

AB	Anchor Bible
AOTC	Abingdon Old Testament Commentary
Bib	*Biblica*
BibInt	*Biblical Interpretation*
BibInt	Biblical Interpretation Series
BibOr	Biblica et Orientalia
FCB	Feminist Companion to the Bible
GBS	Guides to Biblical Scholarship
GPBS	Global Perspectives in Biblical Scholarship
HALOT	Koehler, L., and W. Baumgartner. *The Hebrew and Aramaic Lexicon of the Old Testament.* Translated and edited under the supervision of M. E. J. Richardson. Leiden, 1994-2000.
HCOT	Historical Commentary on the Old Testament
IBC	Interpretation: A Bible Commentary for Teaching and Preaching
ICC	International Critical Commentary
IFT	Introductions in Feminist Theology
JFSR	*Journal of Feminist Studies in Religion*
JPS	Jewish Publication Society

JSOT	*Journal for the Study of the Old Testament*
JSOTSup	Journal for the Study of the Old Testament Supplement Series
LHBOTS	Library of Hebrew Bible/Old Testament Studies
MT	Masoretic Text
NIBC	New International Biblical Commentary
NRSV	New Revised Standard Version
OBT	Overtures to Biblical Theology
SBL	Society of Biblical Literature
SemeiaSt	Semeia Studies
SymS	Symposium Series
THOTC	Two Horizons Old Testament Commentary
WBC	Word Biblical Commentary
ZAW	*Zeitschrift für die alttestamentliche Wissenschaft*

Acknowledgments

Authors are not really the sole creators or originators of a written work. Instead, they are scribes for collective consciousness imprinting in their writing the fruits of conversations, cultural exposures, and the research of others that they have received and synthesized. Indeed, this book is certainly a collation of the ideas and influences of women and men who have gifted me with conversations, their writings, their friendships, and their stories. Some of them I know well, and their encouragement and interest in this work have provided steady support for its completion. The associate dean of my institution, Alison Benders; my colleague Lisa Fullam; and my dear friend Jill Marshall number among those whose regular inquiries about the project provided impetus for steady work on it. The generosity and willingness of those thirteen individuals who provided the Contributing Voices have added a richness and complexity to the work for which I am profoundly grateful. My admiration and gratitude extend also both to Barbara E. Reid, OP, editor of the Wisdom Commentary Series, for conceiving and designing this important project, and to Carol J. Dempsey, OP, for her gracious patience and painstaking work as volume editor of this piece. Others whom I want to thank I know less well or only indirectly from their works. The volumes on Lamentations by Kathleen O'Connor and Adele Berlin proved to be invaluable resources. They often gave me pause and made me wonder if there was anything else to add in excess of their own writings on Lamentations. The impact of their works is everywhere present in this volume, and I owe them both a debt of gratitude for the research and inspiration their works provided.

Without a demanding editor, this project would not have seen the light of day. Hannah Hens-Piazza, my professional editor, who also happens to be my daughter, holds me to the highest standards. My gratitude and admiration for her work ethic, her attention to detail, and her respect for words always increases when we work together. Sarah Kohles, a PhD student at the Graduate Theological Union in Berkeley, deserves a grateful mention as she kindly read through the edited manuscript and gave attention to footnotes. Kelly Miguens was a key player toward the end of the project, graciously reading proofs and helping with subtitles. Her work was of immense importance. I am also indebted to Yoon Kyung Kim and Tae Woong Lee, who provided crucial computer assistance during final editions. As always, my family has been the mainstay in such projects. In particular, my husband, Fred, and my son, Gabriel, provided their regular encouragement and understanding throughout the project, always partaking with me in the satisfaction that comes from such a labor.

Contributors

Dr. Alison M. Benders is associate dean and senior lecturer in systematic theology at the Jesuit School of Theology. She teaches and writes in the areas of sin and justice, receiving the 2016 Association of Catholic Publishers Award for her book *Just Prayer* (Liturgical Press, 2015).

Ms. Kathleen Cooney is a religious studies teacher at Sacred Heart Cathedral Preparatory. A graduate of the master of divinity program at the Jesuit School of Theology, she seeks to find and cultivate inclusive spaces for creative fidelity and dialogue in the Catholic, universal Church.

Ms. Nancy Haught covered religion and ethics for *The Oregonian*, the largest daily newspaper in the Pacific Northwest, for fifteen years. She is working on a book about the sanctity of strangers.

Sr. Sarah Kohles is a Sister of St. Francis of Dubuque, Iowa, and a PhD student at Graduate Theological Union focusing on biblical studies.

Ms. Yoon Kyung Kim is a PhD candidate at the Graduate Theological Union and catechist at San Francisco Grace Presbyterian Church. She is writing a dissertation on the subaltern in biblical narrative.

Ms. Jill Marshall served with the Maryknoll missioners for nine years in Latin America and the United States. She has worked in ministry and education for twenty years. She is currently retired and enjoying being a grandmother.

Ms. Kelly Miguens is currently in her last year in the master of divinity program at the Jesuit School of Theology of Santa Clara University. She has been interning at a federal women's prison in California for the past year, facilitating two classes focused on forgiveness and on women's voices in the Bible.

Dr. Jean Molesky-Poz is lecturer in the Religious Studies Department at Santa Clara University. She lectures, facilitates retreats, and assists groups in developing spirituality study programs.

Dr. Mary Olowin is a psychiatrist who specialized in working with children. In retirement, she is a consultant and trainer for Court Appointed Special Advocates for foster children.

Sr. Anna Pham Phuc, a member of the Daughters of Mary Help of Christians Congregation, is currently director of various hostels for underserved girls in Viet Nam. She also teaches biblical studies to novices in formation and has written several articles focusing on biblical women.

Ms. Sara Prendergast holds a master of divinity from the Jesuit School of Theology of Santa Clara University. She currently teaches Scripture and liturgy courses at St. Ignatius College Preparatory in San Francisco.

Rev. Victor Zhuk, SJ, is a native of Belarus. He holds an STL in biblical studies and is currently teaching spirituality at St Thomas Institute in Moscow.

Foreword

"Tell It on the Mountain"—or, "And You Shall Tell Your Daughter [as Well]"

Athalya Brenner-Idan

Universiteit van Amsterdam/Tel Aviv University

What can Wisdom Commentary do to help, and for whom? The commentary genre has always been privileged in biblical studies. Traditionally acclaimed commentary series, such as the International Critical Commentary, Old Testament and New Testament Library, Hermeneia, Anchor Bible, Eerdmans, and Word—to name but several— enjoy nearly automatic prestige; and the number of women authors who participate in those is relatively small by comparison to their growing number in the scholarly guild. There certainly are some volumes written by women in them, especially in recent decades. At this time, however, this does not reflect the situation on the ground. Further, size matters. In that sense, the sheer size of the Wisdom Commentary is essential. This also represents a considerable investment and the possibility of reaching a wider audience than those already "converted."

Expecting women scholars to deal especially or only with what are considered strictly "female" matters seems unwarranted. According to Audre Lorde, "The master's tools will never dismantle the master's house."[1] But this maxim is not relevant to our case. The point of this commentary is not to destroy but to attain greater participation in the interpretive dialogue about biblical texts. Women scholars may bring additional questions to the readerly agenda as well as fresh angles to existing issues. To assume that their questions are designed only to topple a certain male hegemony is not convincing.

At first I did ask myself: is this commentary series an addition to calm raw nerves, an embellishment to make upholding the old hierarchy palatable? Or is it indeed about becoming the Master? On second and third thoughts, however, I understood that becoming the Master is not what this is about. Knowledge is power. Since Foucault at the very least, this cannot be in dispute. Writing commentaries for biblical texts by women for women and for men, of confessional as well as non-confessional convictions, will sabotage (hopefully) the established hierarchy but will not topple it. This is about an attempt to integrate more fully, to introduce another viewpoint, to become. What excites me about the Wisdom Commentary is that it is not offered as just an alternative supplanting or substituting for the dominant discourse.

These commentaries on biblical books will retain nonauthoritative, pluralistic viewpoints. And yes, once again, the weight of a dedicated series, to distinguish from collections of stand-alone volumes, will prove weightier.

That such an approach is especially important in the case of the Hebrew Bible/Old Testament is beyond doubt. Women of Judaism, Christianity, and also Islam have struggled to make it their own for centuries, even more than they have fought for the New Testament and the Qur'an. Every Hebrew Bible/Old Testament volume in this project is evidence that the day has arrived: it is now possible to read *all* the Jewish canonical books as a collection, for a collection they are, with guidance conceived of with the needs of women readers (not only men) as an integral inspiration and part thereof.

In my Jewish tradition, the main motivation for reciting the Haggadah, the ritual text recited yearly on Passover, the festival of liberation from

---

1. Audre Lorde, "The Master's Tools Will Never Dismantle the Master's House," in *Sister Outsider: Essays and Speeches* (Berkeley, CA: Crossing Press, 1984, 2007), 110–14. First delivered in the Second Sex Conference in New York, 1979.

bondage, is given as "And you shall tell your son" (from Exod 13:8). The knowledge and experience of past generations is thus transferred to the next, for constructing the present and the future. The ancient maxim is, literally, limited to a male audience. This series remolds the maxim into a new inclusive shape, which is of the utmost consequence: "And you shall tell your son" is extended to "And you shall tell your daughter [as well as your son]." Or, if you want, "Tell it on the mountain," for all to hear.

This is what it's all about.

Editor's Introduction to Wisdom Commentary

"She Is a Breath of the Power of God" (Wis 7:25)

Barbara E. Reid, OP

General Editor

Wisdom Commentary is the first series to offer detailed feminist interpretation of every book of the Bible. The fruit of collaborative work by an ecumenical and interreligious team of scholars, the volumes provide serious, scholarly engagement with the whole biblical text, not only those texts that explicitly mention women. The series is intended for clergy, teachers, ministers, and all serious students of the Bible. Designed to be both accessible and informed by the various approaches of biblical scholarship, it pays particular attention to the world in front of the text, that is, how the text is heard and appropriated. At the same time, this series aims to be faithful to the ancient text and its earliest audiences; thus the volumes also explicate the worlds behind the text and within it. While issues of gender are primary in this project, the volumes also address the intersecting issues of power, authority, ethnicity, race, class, and religious belief and practice. The fifty-eight volumes include the books regarded as canonical by Jews (i.e., the Tanakh); Protestants (the "Hebrew Bible" and the New Testament); and Roman Catholic, Anglican, and Eastern

Orthodox Communions (i.e., Tobit, Judith, 1 and 2 Maccabees, Wisdom of Solomon, Sirach/Ecclesiasticus, Baruch, including the Letter of Jeremiah, the additions to Esther, and Susanna and Bel and the Dragon in Daniel).

A Symphony of Diverse Voices

Included in the Wisdom Commentary series are voices from scholars of many different religious traditions, of diverse ages, differing sexual identities, and varying cultural, racial, ethnic, and social contexts. Some have been pioneers in feminist biblical interpretation; others are newer contributors from a younger generation. A further distinctive feature of this series is that each volume incorporates voices other than that of the lead author(s). These voices appear alongside the commentary of the lead author(s), in the grayscale inserts. At times, a contributor may offer an alternative interpretation or a critique of the position taken by the lead author(s). At other times, she or he may offer a complementary interpretation from a different cultural context or subject position. Occasionally, portions of previously published material bring in other views. The diverse voices are not intended to be contestants in a debate or a cacophony of discordant notes. The multiple voices reflect that there is no single definitive feminist interpretation of a text. In addition, they show the importance of subject position in the process of interpretation. In this regard, the Wisdom Commentary series takes inspiration from the Talmud and from *The Torah: A Women's Commentary* (ed. Tamara Cohn Eskenazi and Andrea L. Weiss; New York: Women of Reform Judaism, Federation of Temple Sisterhood, 2008), in which many voices, even conflicting ones, are included and not harmonized.

Contributors include biblical scholars, theologians, and readers of Scripture from outside the scholarly and religious guilds. At times, their comments pertain to a particular text. In some instances they address a theme or topic that arises from the text.

Another feature that highlights the collaborative nature of feminist biblical interpretation is that a number of the volumes have two lead authors who have worked in tandem from the inception of the project and whose voices interweave throughout the commentary.

Woman Wisdom

The title, Wisdom Commentary, reflects both the importance to feminists of the figure of Woman Wisdom in the Scriptures and the distinct wisdom that feminist women and men bring to the interpretive process. In the Scriptures, Woman Wisdom appears as "a breath of the power of God, and a pure emanation of the glory of the Almighty" (Wis 7:25), who was present and active in fashioning all that exists (Prov 8:22-31; Wis 8:6). She is a spirit who pervades and penetrates all things (Wis 7:22-23), and she provides guidance and nourishment at her all-inclusive table (Prov 9:1-5). In both postexilic biblical and nonbiblical Jewish sources, Woman Wisdom is often equated with Torah, e.g., Sirach 24:23-34; Baruch 3:9–4:4; 38:2; 46:4-5; 2 Baruch 48:33, 36; 4 Ezra 5:9-10; 13:55; 14:40; 1 Enoch 42.

The New Testament frequently portrays Jesus as Wisdom incarnate. He invites his followers, "take my yoke upon you and learn from me" (Matt 11:29), just as Ben Sira advises, "put your neck under her [Wisdom's] yoke and let your souls receive instruction" (Sir 51:26). Just as Wisdom experiences rejection (Prov 1:23-25; Sir 15:7-8; Wis 10:3; Bar 3:12), so too does Jesus (Mark 8:31; John 1:10-11). Only some accept his invitation to his all-inclusive banquet (Matt 22:1-14; Luke 14:15-24; compare Prov 1:20-21; 9:3-5). Yet, "wisdom is vindicated by her deeds" (Matt 11:19, speaking of Jesus and John the Baptist; in the Lucan parallel at 7:35 they are called "wisdom's children"). There are numerous parallels between what is said of Wisdom and of the *Logos* in the Prologue of the Fourth Gospel (John 1:1-18). These are only a few of many examples. This female embodiment of divine presence and power is an apt image to guide the work of this series.

Feminism

There are many different understandings of the term "feminism." The various meanings, aims, and methods have developed exponentially in recent decades. Feminism is a perspective and a movement that springs from a recognition of inequities toward women, and it advocates for changes in whatever structures prevent full human flourishing. Three waves of feminism in the United States are commonly recognized. The first, arising in the mid-nineteenth century and lasting into the early twentieth, was sparked by women's efforts to be involved in the public sphere and to win the right to vote. In the 1960s and 1970s, the second wave focused on civil rights and equality for women. With the third wave, from the 1980s forward, came global feminism and the emphasis on the contextual nature of interpretation. Now a fourth wave may be emerging, with a stronger emphasis on the intersectionality of women's concerns with those of other marginalized groups and the increased use of the internet as a platform for discussion and activism.[1] As feminism has matured, it has recognized that inequities based on gender are interwoven with power imbalances based on race, class, ethnicity, religion, sexual identity, physical ability, and a host of other social markers.

Feminist Women and Men

Men who choose to identify with and partner with feminist women in the work of deconstructing systems of domination and building structures of equality are rightly regarded as feminists. Some men readily identify with experiences of women who are discriminated against on the basis of sex/gender, having themselves had comparable experiences; others who may not have faced direct discrimination or stereotyping recognize that inequity and problematic characterization still occur, and they seek correction. This series is pleased to include feminist men both as lead authors and as contributing voices.

Feminist Biblical Interpretation

Women interpreting the Bible from the lenses of their own experience is nothing new. Throughout the ages women have recounted the biblical stories, teaching them to their children and others, all the while interpreting them afresh for their time and circumstances.[2] Following is a very brief sketch of select foremothers who laid the groundwork for contemporary feminist biblical interpretation.

One of the earliest known Christian women who challenged patriarchal interpretations of Scripture was a consecrated virgin named Helie, who lived in the second century CE. When she refused to marry, her

---

1. See Martha Rampton, "Four Waves of Feminism" (October 25, 2015), at http://www.pacificu.edu/about-us/news-events/four-waves-feminism; and Ealasaid Munro, "Feminism: A Fourth Wave?," https://www.psa.ac.uk/insight-plus/feminism-fourth-wave.

2. For fuller treatments of this history, see chap. 7, "One Thousand Years of Feminist Bible Criticism," in Gerda Lerner, *Creation of Feminist Consciousness: From the Middle Ages to Eighteen-Seventy* (New York: Oxford University Press, 1993), 138–66; Susanne Scholz, "From the 'Woman's Bible' to the 'Women's Bible,' The History of Feminist Approaches to the Hebrew Bible," in *Introducing the Women's Hebrew Bible*, IFT 13 (New York: T&T Clark, 2007), 12–32; Marion Ann Taylor and Agnes Choi, eds., *Handbook of Women Biblical Interpreters: A Historical and Biographical Guide* (Grand Rapids: Baker Academic, 2012).

parents brought her before a judge, who quoted to her Paul's admonition, "It is better to marry than to be aflame with passion" (1 Cor 7:9). In response, Helie first acknowledges that this is what Scripture says, but then she retorts, "but not for everyone, that is, not for holy virgins."[3] She is one of the first to question the notion that a text has one meaning that is applicable in all situations.

A Jewish woman who also lived in the second century CE, Beruriah, is said to have had "profound knowledge of biblical exegesis and outstanding intelligence."[4] One story preserved in the Talmud (b. Berakot 10a) tells of how she challenged her husband, Rabbi Meir, when he prayed for the destruction of a sinner. Proffering an alternate interpretation, she argued that Psalm 104:35 advocated praying for the destruction of sin, not the sinner.

In medieval times the first written commentaries on Scripture from a critical feminist point of view emerge. While others may have been produced and passed on orally, they are for the most part lost to us now. Among the earliest preserved feminist writings are those of Hildegard of Bingen (1098–1179), German writer, mystic, and abbess of a Benedictine monastery. She reinterpreted the Genesis narratives in a way that presented women and men as complementary and interdependent. She frequently wrote about feminine aspects of the Divine.[5] Along with other women mystics of the time, such as Julian of Norwich (1342–ca. 1416), she spoke authoritatively from her personal experiences of God's revelation in prayer.

In this era, women were also among the scribes who copied biblical manuscripts. Notable among them is Paula Dei Mansi of Verona, from a distinguished family of Jewish scribes. In 1288, she translated from Hebrew into Italian a collection of Bible commentaries written by her father and added her own explanations.[6]

Another pioneer, Christine de Pizan (1365–ca. 1430), was a French court writer and prolific poet. She used allegory and common sense

---

3. Madrid, Escorial MS, a II 9, f. 90 v., as cited in Lerner, *Feminist Consciousness*, 140.

4. See Judith R. Baskin, "Women and Post-Biblical Commentary," in *The Torah: A Women's Commentary*, ed. Tamara Cohn Eskenazi and Andrea L. Weiss (New York: Women of Reform Judaism, Federation of Temple Sisterhood, 2008), xlix–lv, at lii.

5. Hildegard of Bingen, *De Operatione Dei*, 1.4.100; PL 197:885bc, as cited in Lerner, *Feminist Consciousness*, 142–43. See also Barbara Newman, *Sister of Wisdom: St. Hildegard's Theology of the Feminine* (Berkeley: University of California Press, 1987).

6. Emily Taitz, Sondra Henry, Cheryl Tallan, eds., *JPS Guide to Jewish Women 600 B.C.E.–1900 C.E.* (Philadelphia: Jewish Publication Society of America, 2003), 110–11.

to subvert misogynist readings of Scripture and celebrated the accomplishments of female biblical figures to argue for women's active roles in building society.[7]

By the seventeenth century, there were women who asserted that the biblical text needs to be understood and interpreted in its historical context. For example, Rachel Speght (1597–ca. 1630), a Calvinist English poet, elaborates on the historical situation in first-century Corinth that prompted Paul to say, "It is well for a man not to touch a woman" (1 Cor 7:1). Her aim was to show that the biblical texts should not be applied in a literal fashion to all times and circumstances. Similarly, Margaret Fell (1614–1702), one of the founders of the Religious Society of Friends (Quakers) in Britain, addressed the Pauline prohibitions against women speaking in church by insisting that they do not have universal validity. Rather, they need to be understood in their historical context, as addressed to a local church in particular time-bound circumstances.[8]

Along with analyzing the historical context of the biblical writings, women in the eighteenth and nineteenth centuries began to attend to misogynistic interpretations based on faulty translations. One of the first to do so was British feminist Mary Astell (1666–1731).[9] In the United States, the Grimké sisters, Sarah (1792–1873) and Angelina (1805–1879), Quaker women from a slaveholding family in South Carolina, learned biblical Greek and Hebrew so that they could interpret the Bible for themselves. They were prompted to do so after men sought to silence them from speaking out against slavery and for women's rights by claiming that the Bible (e.g., 1 Cor 14:34) prevented women from speaking in public.[10] Another prominent abolitionist, Sojourner Truth (ca. 1797–1883), a former slave, quoted the Bible liberally in her speeches[11] and in so doing challenged cultural assumptions and biblical interpretations that undergird gender inequities.

---

7. See further Taylor and Choi, *Handbook of Women Biblical Interpreters*, 127–32.

8. Her major work, *Women's Speaking Justified, Proved and Allowed by the Scriptures*, published in London in 1667, gave a systematic feminist reading of all biblical texts pertaining to women.

9. Mary Astell, *Some Reflections upon Marriage* (New York: Source Book Press, 1970, reprint of the 1730 edition; earliest edition of this work is 1700), 103–4.

10. See further Sarah Grimké, *Letters on the Equality of the Sexes and the Condition of Woman* (Boston: Isaac Knapp, 1838).

11. See, for example, her most famous speech, "Ain't I a Woman?," delivered in 1851 at the Ohio Women's Rights Convention in Akron, OH; http://www.fordham.edu/halsall/mod/sojtruth-woman.asp.

Another monumental work that emerged in nineteenth-century England was that of Jewish theologian Grace Aguilar (1816–1847), *The Women of Israel*,[12] published in 1845. Aguilar's approach was to make connections between the biblical women and contemporary Jewish women's concerns. She aimed to counter the widespread notion that women were degraded in Jewish law and that only in Christianity were women's dignity and value upheld. Her intent was to help Jewish women find strength and encouragement by seeing the evidence of God's compassionate love in the history of every woman in the Bible. While not a full commentary on the Bible, Aguilar's work stands out for its comprehensive treatment of every female biblical character, including even the most obscure references.[13]

The first person to produce a full-blown feminist commentary on the Bible was Elizabeth Cady Stanton (1815–1902). A leading proponent in the United States for women's right to vote, she found that whenever women tried to make inroads into politics, education, or the work world, the Bible was quoted against them. Along with a team of like-minded women, she produced her own commentary on every text of the Bible that concerned women. Her pioneering two-volume project, *The Woman's Bible*, published in 1895 and 1898, urges women to recognize that texts that degrade women come from the men who wrote the texts, not from God, and to use their common sense to rethink what has been presented to them as sacred.

Nearly a century later, *The Women's Bible Commentary*, edited by Carol Newsom and Sharon Ringe (Louisville: Westminster John Knox, 1992), appeared. This one-volume commentary features North American feminist scholarship on each book of the Protestant canon. Like Cady Stanton's commentary, it does not contain comments on every section of the biblical text but only on those passages deemed relevant to women. It was revised and expanded in 1998 to include the Apocrypha/Deuterocanonical books, and the contributors to this new volume reflect the global face of contemporary feminist scholarship. The revisions made in the third edition, which appeared in 2012, represent the profound advances in feminist biblical scholarship and include newer voices. In both the second and third editions, *The* has been dropped from the title.

---

12. The full title is *The Women of Israel or Characters and Sketches from the Holy Scriptures and Jewish History Illustrative of the Past History, Present Duty, and Future Destiny of the Hebrew Females, as Based on the Word of God.*

13. See further Eskenazi and Weiss, *The Torah: A Women's Commentary*, xxxviii; Taylor and Choi, *Handbook of Women Biblical Interpreters*, 31–37.

Also appearing at the centennial of Cady Stanton's *The Woman's Bible* were two volumes edited by Elisabeth Schüssler Fiorenza with the assistance of Shelly Matthews. The first, *Searching the Scriptures: A Feminist Introduction* (New York: Crossroad, 1993), charts a comprehensive approach to feminist interpretation from ecumenical, interreligious, and multicultural perspectives. The second volume, published in 1994, provides critical feminist commentary on each book of the New Testament as well as on three books of Jewish Pseudepigrapha and eleven other early Christian writings.

In Europe, similar endeavors have been undertaken, such as the one-volume *Kompendium Feministische Bibelauslegung*, edited by Luise Schottroff and Marie-Theres Wacker (Gütersloh: Gütersloher Verlagshaus, 2007), featuring German feminist biblical interpretation of each book of the Bible, along with apocryphal books, and several extrabiblical writings. This work, now in its third edition, has recently been translated into English.[14] A multivolume project, *The Bible and Women: An Encyclopaedia of Exegesis and Cultural History*, edited by Irmtraud Fischer, Adriana Valerio, Mercedes Navarro Puerto, and Christiana de Groot, is currently in production. This project presents a history of the reception of the Bible as embedded in Western cultural history and focuses particularly on gender-relevant biblical themes, biblical female characters, and women recipients of the Bible. The volumes are published in English, Spanish, Italian, and German.[15]

Another groundbreaking work is the collection The Feminist Companion to the Bible Series, edited by Athalya Brenner (Sheffield: Sheffield Academic, 1993–2015), which comprises twenty volumes of commen-

---

14. *Feminist Biblical Interpretation: A Compendium of Critical Commentary on the Books of the Bible and Related Literature*, trans. Lisa E. Dahill, Everett R. Kalin, Nancy Lukens, Linda M. Maloney, Barbara Rumscheidt, Martin Rumscheidt, and Tina Steiner (Grand Rapids: Eerdmans, 2012). Another notable collection is the three volumes edited by Susanne Scholz, *Feminist Interpretation of the Hebrew Bible in Retrospect*, Recent Research in Biblical Studies 7, 8, 9 (Sheffield: Sheffield Phoenix, 2013, 2014, 2016).

15. The first volume, on the Torah, appeared in Spanish in 2009, in German and Italian in 2010, and in English in 2011 (Atlanta: SBL Press). Four more volumes are now available: *Feminist Biblical Studies in the Twentieth Century*, ed. Elisabeth Schüssler Fiorenza (2014); *The Writings and Later Wisdom Books*, ed. Christl M. Maier and Nuria Calduch-Benages (2014); *Gospels: Narrative and History*, ed. Mercedes Navarro Puerto, Marinella Perroni, and Amy-Jill Levine (2015); and *The High Middle Ages*, ed. Kari Elisabeth Børresen and Adriana Valerio (2015). For further information, see http://www.bibleandwomen.org.

taries on the Old Testament. The parallel series, Feminist Companion to the New Testament and Early Christian Writings, edited by Amy-Jill Levine with Marianne Blickenstaff and Maria Mayo Robbins (Sheffield: Sheffield Academic, 2001–2009), contains thirteen volumes with one more planned. These two series are not full commentaries on the biblical books but comprise collected essays on discrete biblical texts.

Works by individual feminist biblical scholars in all parts of the world abound, and they are now too numerous to list in this introduction. Feminist biblical interpretation has reached a level of maturity that now makes possible a commentary series on every book of the Bible. In recent decades, women have had greater access to formal theological education, have been able to learn critical analytical tools, have put their own interpretations into writing, and have developed new methods of biblical interpretation. Until recent decades the work of feminist biblical interpreters was largely unknown, both to other women and to their brothers in the synagogue, church, and academy. Feminists now have taken their place in the professional world of biblical scholars, where they build on the work of their foremothers and connect with one another across the globe in ways not previously possible. In a few short decades, feminist biblical criticism has become an integral part of the academy.

Methodologies

Feminist biblical scholars use a variety of methods and often employ a number of them together.[16] In the Wisdom Commentary series, the authors will explain their understanding of feminism and the feminist reading strategies used in their commentary. Each volume treats the biblical text in blocks of material, not an analysis verse by verse. The entire text is considered, not only those passages that feature female characters or that speak specifically about women. When women are not apparent in the narrative, feminist lenses are used to analyze the dynamics in the text between male characters, the models of power, binary ways of thinking, and dynamics of imperialism. Attention is given to how the whole text functions and how it was and is heard, both in its original context and today. Issues of particular concern to women—e.g., poverty, food, health, the environment, water—come to the fore.

---

16. See the seventeen essays in Caroline Vander Stichele and Todd Penner, eds., *Her Master's Tools? Feminist and Postcolonial Engagements of Historical-Critical Discourse* (Atlanta: SBL Press, 2005), which show the complementarity of various approaches.

One of the approaches used by early feminists and still popular today is to lift up the overlooked and forgotten stories of women in the Bible. Studies of women in each of the Testaments have been done, and there are also studies on women in particular biblical books.[17] Feminists recognize that the examples of biblical characters can be both empowering and problematic. The point of the feminist enterprise is not to serve as an apologetic for women; it is rather, in part, to recover women's history and literary roles in all their complexity and to learn from that recovery.

Retrieving the submerged history of biblical women is a crucial step for constructing the story of the past so as to lead to liberative possibilities for the present and future. There are, however, some pitfalls to this approach. Sometimes depictions of biblical women have been naïve and romantic. Some commentators exalt the virtues of both biblical and contemporary women and paint women as superior to men. Such reverse discrimination inhibits movement toward equality for all. In addition, some feminists challenge the idea that one can "pluck positive images out of an admittedly androcentric text, separating literary characterizations from the androcentric interests they were created to serve."[18] Still other feminists find these images to have enormous value.

One other danger with seeking the submerged history of women is the tendency for Christian feminists to paint Jesus and even Paul as liberators of women in a way that demonizes Judaism.[19] Wisdom Commentary aims to enhance understanding of Jesus as well as Paul as Jews of their day and to forge solidarity among Jewish and Christian feminists.

---

17. See, e.g., Alice Bach, ed., *Women in the Hebrew Bible: A Reader* (New York: Routledge, 1998); Tikva Frymer-Kensky, *Reading the Women of the Bible* (New York: Schocken Books, 2002); Carol Meyers, Toni Craven, and Ross S. Kraemer, *Women in Scripture* (Grand Rapids: Eerdmans, 2000); Irene Nowell, *Women in the Old Testament* (Collegeville, MN: Liturgical Press, 1997); Katharine Doob Sakenfeld, *Just Wives? Stories of Power and Survival in the Old Testament and Today* (Louisville: Westminster John Knox, 2003); Mary Ann Getty-Sullivan, *Women in the New Testament* (Collegeville, MN: Liturgical Press, 2001); Bonnie Thurston, *Women in the New Testament: Questions and Commentary*, Companions to the New Testament (New York: Crossroad, 1998).

18. Cheryl Exum, "Second Thoughts about Secondary Characters: Women in Exodus 1.8–2.10," in *A Feminist Companion to Exodus to Deuteronomy*, FCB 6, ed. Athalya Brenner (Sheffield: Sheffield Academic, 1994), 75–97, at 76.

19. See Judith Plaskow, "Anti-Judaism in Feminist Christian Interpretation," in *Searching the Scriptures: A Feminist Introduction*, ed. Elisabeth Schüssler Fiorenza (New York: Crossroad, 1993), 1:117–29; Amy-Jill Levine, "The New Testament and Anti-Judaism," in *The Misunderstood Jew: The Church and the Scandal of the Jewish Jesus* (San Francisco: HarperSanFrancisco, 2006), 87–117.

Feminist scholars who use historical-critical methods analyze the world behind the text; they seek to understand the historical context from which the text emerged and the circumstances of the communities to whom it was addressed. In bringing feminist lenses to this approach, the aim is not to impose modern expectations on ancient cultures but to unmask the ways that ideologically problematic mind-sets that produced the ancient texts are still promulgated through the text. Feminist biblical scholars aim not only to deconstruct but also to reclaim and reconstruct biblical history as women's history, in which women were central and active agents in creating religious heritage.[20] A further step is to construct meaning for contemporary women and men in a liberative movement toward transformation of social, political, economic, and religious structures.[21] In recent years, some feminists have embraced new historicism, which accents the creative role of the interpreter in any construction of history and exposes the power struggles to which the text witnesses.[22]

Literary critics analyze the world of the text: its form, language patterns, and rhetorical function.[23] They do not attempt to separate layers of tradition and redaction but focus on the text holistically, as it is in

20. See, for example, Phyllis A. Bird, *Missing Persons and Mistaken Identities: Women and Gender in Ancient Israel* (Minneapolis: Fortress, 1997); Elisabeth Schüssler Fiorenza, *In Memory of Her: A Feminist Theological Reconstruction of Christian Origins* (New York: Crossroad, 1984); Ross Shepard Kraemer and Mary Rose D'Angelo, eds., *Women and Christian Origins* (New York: Oxford University Press, 1999).

21. See, e.g., Sandra M. Schneiders, *The Revelatory Text: Interpreting the New Testament as Sacred Scripture*, rev. ed. (Collegeville, MN: Liturgical Press, 1999), whose aim is to engage in biblical interpretation not only for intellectual enlightenment but, even more important, for personal and communal transformation. Elisabeth Schüssler Fiorenza (*Wisdom Ways: Introducing Feminist Biblical Interpretation* [Maryknoll, NY: Orbis Books, 2001]) envisions the work of feminist biblical interpretation as a dance of Wisdom that consists of seven steps that interweave in spiral movements toward liberation, the final one being transformative action for change.

22. See Gina Hens-Piazza, *The New Historicism*, GBS, Old Testament Series (Minneapolis: Fortress, 2002).

23. Phyllis Trible was among the first to employ this method with texts from Genesis and Ruth in her groundbreaking book *God and the Rhetoric of Sexuality*, OBT (Philadelphia: Fortress, 1978). Another pioneer in feminist literary criticism is Mieke Bal (*Lethal Love: Feminist Literary Readings of Biblical Love Stories* [Bloomington: Indiana University Press, 1987]). For surveys of recent developments in literary methods, see Terry Eagleton, *Literary Theory: An Introduction*, 3rd ed. (Minneapolis: University of Minnesota Press, 2008); Janice Capel Anderson and Stephen D. Moore, eds., *Mark and Method: New Approaches in Biblical Studies*, 2nd ed. (Minneapolis: Fortress, 2008).

its present form. They examine how meaning is created in the interaction between the text and its reader in multiple contexts. Within the arena of literary approaches are reader-oriented approaches, narrative, rhetorical, structuralist, post-structuralist, deconstructive, ideological, autobiographical, and performance criticism.[24] Narrative critics study the interrelation among author, text, and audience through investigation of settings, both spatial and temporal; characters; plot; and narrative techniques (e.g., irony, parody, intertextual allusions). Reader-response critics attend to the impact that the text has on the reader or hearer. They recognize that when a text is detrimental toward women there is the choice either to affirm the text or to read against the grain toward a liberative end. Rhetorical criticism analyzes the style of argumentation and attends to how the author is attempting to shape the thinking or actions of the hearer. Structuralist critics analyze the complex patterns of binary oppositions in the text to derive its meaning.[25] Post-structuralist approaches challenge the notion that there are fixed meanings to any biblical text or that there is one universal truth. They engage in close readings of the text and often engage in intertextual analysis.[26] Within this approach is deconstructionist criticism, which views the text as a site of conflict, with competing narratives. The interpreter aims to expose the fault lines and overturn and reconfigure binaries by elevating the underling of a pair and foregrounding it.[27] Feminists also use other post-modern approaches, such as ideological and autobiographical criticism. The former analyzes the system of ideas that underlies the power and

24. See, e.g., J. Cheryl Exum and David J. A. Clines, eds., *The New Literary Criticism and the Hebrew Bible* (Valley Forge, PA: Trinity Press International, 1993); Edgar V. McKnight and Elizabeth Struthers Malbon, eds., *The New Literary Criticism and the New Testament* (Valley Forge, PA: Trinity Press International, 1994).

25. See, e.g., David Jobling, *The Sense of Biblical Narrative: Three Structural Analyses in the Old Testament*, JSOTSup 7 (Sheffield: University of Sheffield, 1978).

26. See, e.g., Stephen D. Moore, *Poststructuralism and the New Testament: Derrida and Foucault at the Foot of the Cross* (Minneapolis: Fortress, 1994); *The Bible in Theory: Critical and Postcritical Essays* (Atlanta: SBL Press, 2010); Yvonne Sherwood, *A Biblical Text and Its Afterlives: The Survival of Jonah in Western Culture* (Cambridge: Cambridge University Press, 2000).

27. David Penchansky, "Deconstruction," in *The Oxford Encyclopedia of Biblical Interpretation*, ed. Steven McKenzie (New York: Oxford University Press, 2013), 196–205. See, for example, Danna Nolan Fewell and David M. Gunn, *Gender, Power, and Promise: The Subject of the Bible's First Story* (Nashville: Abingdon, 1993); David Rutledge, *Reading Marginally: Feminism, Deconstruction and the Bible*, BibInt 21 (Leiden: Brill, 1996).

values concealed in the text as well as that of the interpreter.[28] The latter involves deliberate self-disclosure while reading the text as a critical exegete.[29] Performance criticism attends to how the text was passed on orally, usually in communal settings, and to the verbal and nonverbal interactions between the performer and the audience.[30]

From the beginning, feminists have understood that interpreting the Bible is an act of power. In recent decades, feminist biblical scholars have developed hermeneutical theories of the ethics and politics of biblical interpretation to challenge the claims to value neutrality of most academic biblical scholarship. Feminist biblical scholars have also turned their attention to how some biblical writings were shaped by the power of empire and how this still shapes readers' self-understandings today. They have developed hermeneutical approaches that reveal, critique, and evaluate the interactions depicted in the text against the context of empire, and they consider implications for contemporary contexts.[31] Feminists also analyze the dynamics of colonization and the mentalities of colonized peoples in the exercise of biblical interpretation. As Kwok Pui-lan explains, "A postcolonial feminist interpretation of the Bible needs to investigate the deployment of gender in the narration of identity, the negotiation of power differentials between the colonizers and the colonized, and the reinforcement of patriarchal control over spheres where these elites could exercise control."[32] Methods and models from sociology and cultural anthropology are used by feminists to investigate

28. See Tina Pippin, ed., *Ideological Criticism of Biblical Texts: Semeia* 59 (1992); Terry Eagleton, *Ideology: An Introduction* (London: Verso, 2007).

29. See, e.g., Ingrid Rose Kitzberger, ed., *Autobiographical Biblical Interpretation: Between Text and Self* (Leiden: Deo, 2002); P. J. W. Schutte, "When *They, We*, and the Passive Become *I*—Introducing Autobiographical Biblical Criticism," *HTS Teologiese Studies / Theological Studies* 61 (2005): 401–16.

30. See, e.g., Holly Hearon and Philip Ruge-Jones, eds., *The Bible in Ancient and Modern Media: Story and Performance* (Eugene, OR: Cascade, 2009).

31. E.g., Gale Yee, ed., *Judges and Method: New Approaches in Biblical Studies* (Minneapolis: Fortress, 1995); Warren Carter, *The Gospel of Matthew in Its Roman Imperial Context* (London: T&T Clark, 2005); *The Roman Empire and the New Testament: An Essential Guide* (Nashville: Abingdon, 2006); Elisabeth Schüssler Fiorenza, *The Power of the Word: Scripture and the Rhetoric of Empire* (Minneapolis: Fortress, 2007); Judith E. McKinlay, *Reframing Her: Biblical Women in Postcolonial Focus* (Sheffield: Sheffield Phoenix, 2004).

32. Kwok Pui-lan, *Postcolonial Imagination and Feminist Theology* (Louisville: Westminster John Knox, 2005), 9. See also, Musa W. Dube, ed., *Postcolonial Feminist Interpretation of the Bible* (St. Louis: Chalice, 2000); Cristl M. Maier and Carolyn J. Sharp,

women's everyday lives, their experiences of marriage, childrearing, labor, money, illness, etc.[33]

As feminists have examined the construction of gender from varying cultural perspectives, they have become ever more cognizant that the way gender roles are defined within differing cultures varies radically. As Mary Ann Tolbert observes, "Attempts to isolate some universal role that cross-culturally defines 'woman' have run into contradictory evidence at every turn."[34] Some women have coined new terms to highlight the particularities of their socio-cultural context. Many African American feminists, for example, call themselves *womanists* to draw attention to the double oppression of racism and sexism they experience.[35] Similarly, many US Hispanic feminists speak of themselves as *mujeristas* (*mujer* is Spanish for "woman").[36] Others prefer to be called "Latina feminists."[37] Both groups emphasize that the context for their theologizing is *mestizaje* and *mulatez* (racial and cultural mixture), done *en conjunto* (in community), with *lo cotidiano* (everyday lived experience) of Hispanic women as starting points for theological reflection and the encounter with the divine. Intercultural analysis has become an indispensable tool for working toward justice for women at the global level.[38]

Prophecy and Power: Jeremiah in Feminist and Postcolonial Perspective (London: Bloomsbury, 2013).

33. See, for example, Carol Meyers, *Discovering Eve: Ancient Israelite Women in Context* (New York: Oxford University Press, 1991); Luise Schottroff, *Lydia's Impatient Sisters: A Feminist Social History of Early Christianity*, trans. Barbara and Martin Rumscheidt (Louisville: Westminster John Knox, 1995); Susan Niditch, *"My Brother Esau Is a Hairy Man": Hair and Identity in Ancient Israel* (Oxford: Oxford University Press, 2008).

34. Mary Ann Tolbert, "Social, Sociological, and Anthropological Methods," in *Searching the Scriptures*, 1:255–71, at 265.

35. Alice Walker coined the term (*In Search of Our Mothers' Gardens: Womanist Prose* [New York: Harcourt Brace Jovanovich, 1967, 1983]). See also Katie G. Cannon, "The Emergence of Black Feminist Consciousness," in *Feminist Interpretation of the Bible*, ed. Letty M. Russell (Philadelphia: Westminster, 1985), 30–40; Renita Weems, *Just a Sister Away: A Womanist Vision of Women's Relationships in the Bible* (San Diego: Lura Media, 1988); Nyasha Junior, *An Introduction to Womanist Biblical Interpretation* (Louisville: Westminster John Knox, 2015).

36. Ada María Isasi-Díaz (*Mujerista Theology: A Theology for the Twenty-First Century* [Maryknoll, NY: Orbis Books, 1996]) is credited with coining the term.

37. E.g., María Pilar Aquino, Daisy L. Machado, and Jeanette Rodríguez, eds., *A Reader in Latina Feminist Theology* (Austin: University of Texas Press, 2002).

38. See, e.g., María Pilar Aquino and María José Rosado-Nunes, eds., *Feminist Intercultural Theology: Latina Explorations for a Just World*, Studies in Latino/a Catholicism

Some feminists are among those who have developed lesbian, gay, bisexual, and transgender (LGBT) interpretation. This approach focuses on issues of sexual identity and uses various reading strategies. Some point out the ways in which categories that emerged in recent centuries are applied anachronistically to biblical texts to make modern-day judgments. Others show how the Bible is silent on contemporary issues about sexual identity. Still others examine same-sex relationships in the Bible by figures such as Ruth and Naomi or David and Jonathan. In recent years, queer theory has emerged; it emphasizes the blurriness of boundaries not just of sexual identity but also of gender roles. Queer critics often focus on texts in which figures transgress what is traditionally considered proper gender behavior.[39]

Feminists also recognize that the struggle for women's equality and dignity is intimately connected with the struggle for respect for Earth and for the whole of the cosmos. Ecofeminists interpret Scripture in ways that highlight the link between human domination of nature and male subjugation of women. They show how anthropocentric ways of interpreting the Bible have overlooked or dismissed Earth and Earth community. They invite readers to identify not only with human characters in the biblical narrative but also with other Earth creatures and domains of nature, especially those that are the object of injustice. Some use creative imagination to retrieve the interests of Earth implicit in the narrative and enable Earth to speak.[40]

Biblical Authority

By the late nineteenth century, some feminists, such as Elizabeth Cady Stanton, began to question openly whether the Bible could continue to be regarded as authoritative for women. They viewed the Bible itself as

---

(Maryknoll, NY: Orbis Books, 2007).

39. See, e.g., Bernadette J. Brooten, *Love between Women: Early Christian Responses to Female Homoeroticism* (Chicago and London: University of Chicago Press, 1996); Mary Rose D'Angelo, "Women Partners in the New Testament," *JFSR* 6 (1990): 65–86; Deirdre J. Good, "Reading Strategies for Biblical Passages on Same-Sex Relations," *Theology and Sexuality* 7 (1997): 70–82; Deryn Guest, *When Deborah Met Jael: Lesbian Feminist Hermeneutics* (London: SCM, 2011); Teresa Hornsby and Ken Stone, eds., *Bible Trouble: Queer Readings at the Boundaries of Biblical Scholarship* (Atlanta: SBL Press, 2011).

40. E.g., Norman C. Habel and Peter Trudinger, *Exploring Ecological Hermeneutics*, SymS 46 (Atlanta: SBL Press, 2008); Mary Judith Ress, *Ecofeminism in Latin America*, Women from the Margins (Maryknoll, NY: Orbis Books, 2006).

the source of women's oppression, and some rejected its sacred origin and saving claims. Some decided that the Bible and the religious traditions that enshrine it are too thoroughly saturated with androcentrism and patriarchy to be redeemable.[41]

In the Wisdom Commentary series, questions such as these may be raised, but the aim of this series is not to lead readers to reject the authority of the biblical text. Rather, the aim is to promote better understanding of the contexts from which the text arose and of the rhetorical effects it has on women and men in contemporary contexts. Such understanding can lead to a deepening of faith, with the Bible serving as an aid to bring flourishing of life.

Language for God

Because of the ways in which the term "God" has been used to symbolize the divine in predominantly male, patriarchal, and monarchical modes, feminists have designed new ways of speaking of the divine. Some have called attention to the inadequacy of the term *God* by trying to visually destabilize our ways of thinking and speaking of the divine. Rosemary Radford Ruether proposed *God/ess*, as an unpronounceable term pointing to the unnameable understanding of the divine that transcends patriarchal limitations.[42] Some have followed traditional Jewish practice, writing *G-d*. Elisabeth Schüssler Fiorenza has adopted *G*d*.[43] Others draw on the biblical tradition to mine female and non-gender-specific metaphors and symbols.[44] In Wisdom Commentary, there is not one standard way of expressing the divine; each author will use her or his preferred ways. The one exception is that when the tetragrammaton, YHWH, the name revealed to Moses in Exodus 3:14, is used, it will be without vowels, respecting the Jewish custom of avoiding pronouncing the divine name out of reverence.

---

41. E.g., Mary Daly, *Beyond God the Father: A Philosophy of Women's Liberation* (Boston: Beacon, 1973).

42. Rosemary Radford Ruether, *Sexism and God-Talk: Toward a Feminist Theology* (Boston: Beacon, 1983).

43. Elisabeth Schüssler Fiorenza, *Jesus: Miriam's Child, Sophia's Prophet; Critical Issues in Feminist Christology* (New York: Continuum, 1994), 191 n. 3.

44. E.g., Sallie McFague, *Models of God: Theology for an Ecological, Nuclear Age* (Philadelphia: Fortress, 1987); Catherine LaCugna, *God for Us: The Trinity and Christian Life* (San Francisco: Harper Collins, 1991); Elizabeth A. Johnson, *She Who Is: The Mystery of God in Feminist Theological Discourse* (New York: Crossroad, 1992). See further Elizabeth A. Johnson, "God," in *Dictionary of Feminist Theologies*, 128–30.

Nomenclature for the Two Testaments

In recent decades, some biblical scholars have begun to call the two Testaments of the Bible by names other than the traditional nomenclature: Old and New Testament. Some regard "Old" as derogatory, implying that it is no longer relevant or that it has been superseded. Consequently, terms like Hebrew Bible, First Testament, and Jewish Scriptures and, correspondingly, Christian Scriptures or Second Testament have come into use. There are a number of difficulties with these designations. The term "Hebrew Bible" does not take into account that parts of the Old Testament are written not in Hebrew but in Aramaic.[45] Moreover, for Roman Catholics and Eastern Orthodox believers, the Old Testament includes books written in Greek—the Deuterocanonical books, considered Apocrypha by Protestants.[46] The term "Jewish Scriptures" is inadequate because these books are also sacred to Christians. Conversely, "Christian Scriptures" is not an accurate designation for the New Testament, since the Old Testament is also part of the Christian Scriptures. Using "First and Second Testament" also has difficulties, in that it can imply a hierarchy and a value judgment.[47] Jews generally use the term Tanakh, an acronym for Torah (Pentateuch), Nevi'im (Prophets), and Ketuvim (Writings).

In Wisdom Commentary, if authors choose to use a designation other than Tanakh, Old Testament, and New Testament, they will explain how they mean the term.

Translation

Modern feminist scholars recognize the complexities connected with biblical translation, as they have delved into questions about philosophy of language, how meanings are produced, and how they are culturally situated. Today it is evident that simply translating into gender-neutral formulations cannot address all the challenges presented by androcentric texts. Efforts at feminist translation must also deal with issues around authority and canonicity.[48]

---

45. Gen 31:47; Jer 10:11; Ezra 4:7–6:18; 7:12-26; Dan 2:4–7:28.

46. Representing the *via media* between Catholic and reformed, Anglicans generally consider the Apocrypha to be profitable, if not canonical, and utilize select Wisdom texts liturgically.

47. See Levine, *The Misunderstood Jew*, 193–99.

48. Elizabeth Castelli, "*Les Belles Infidèles*/Fidelity or Feminism? The Meanings of Feminist Biblical Translation," in *Searching the Scriptures*, 1:189–204, here 190.

Because of these complexities, the editors of Wisdom Commentary series have chosen to use an existing translation, the New Revised Standard Version (NRSV), which is provided for easy reference at the top of each page of commentary. The NRSV was produced by a team of ecumenical and interreligious scholars, is a fairly literal translation, and uses inclusive language for human beings. Brief discussions about problematic translations appear in the inserts labeled "Translation Matters." When more detailed discussions are available, these will be indicated in footnotes. In the commentary, wherever Hebrew or Greek words are used, English translation is provided. In cases where a wordplay is involved, transliteration is provided to enable understanding.

Art and Poetry

Artistic expression in poetry, music, sculpture, painting, and various other modes is very important to feminist interpretation. Where possible, art and poetry are included in the print volumes of the series. In a number of instances, these are original works created for this project. Regrettably, copyright and production costs prohibit the inclusion of color photographs and other artistic work. It is our hope that the web version will allow a greater collection of such resources.

Glossary

Because there are a number of excellent readily available resources that provide definitions and concise explanations of terms used in feminist theological and biblical studies, this series will not include a glossary. We refer you to works such as *Dictionary of Feminist Theologies*, edited by Letty M. Russell with J. Shannon Clarkson (Louisville: Westminster John Knox, 1996), and volume 1 of *Searching the Scriptures*, edited by Elisabeth Schüssler Fiorenza with the assistance of Shelly Matthews (New York: Crossroad, 1992). Individual authors in the Wisdom Commentary series will define the way they are using terms that may be unfamiliar.

Bibliography

Because bibliographies are quickly outdated and because the space is limited, only a list of Works Cited is included in the print volumes. A comprehensive bibliography for each volume is posted on a dedicated website and is updated regularly. The link for this volume can be found at wisdomcommentary.org.

A Concluding Word

In just a few short decades, feminist biblical studies has grown exponentially, both in the methods that have been developed and in the number of scholars who have embraced it. We realize that this series is limited and will soon need to be revised and updated. It is our hope that Wisdom Commentary, by making the best of current feminist biblical scholarship available in an accessible format to ministers, preachers, teachers, scholars, and students, will aid all readers in their advancement toward God's vision of dignity, equality, and justice for all.

━━◆━━

Acknowledgments

There are a great many people who have made this series possible: first, Peter Dwyer, director of Liturgical Press, and Hans Christoffersen, publisher of the academic market at Liturgical Press, who have believed in this project and have shepherded it since it was conceived in 2008. Editorial consultants Athalya Brenner-Idan and Elisabeth Schüssler Fiorenza have not only been an inspiration with their pioneering work but also have encouraged us all along the way with their personal involvement. Volume editors Mary Ann Beavis, Carol J. Dempsey, Amy-Jill Levine, Linda M. Maloney, Ahida Pilarski, Sarah Tanzer, Lauress Wilkins Lawrence, and Seung Ai Yang have lent their extraordinary wisdom to the shaping of the series, have used their extensive networks of relationships to secure authors and contributors, and have worked tirelessly to guide their work to completion. Two others who contributed greatly to the shaping of the project at the outset were Linda M. Day and Mignon Jacobs, as well as Barbara E. Bowe of blessed memory (d. 2010). Editorial and research assistant Susan M. Hickman has provided invaluable support with administrative details and arrangements. I am grateful to Brian Eisenschenk and Christine Henderson who have assisted Susan Hickman with the Wiki. There are countless others at Liturgical Press whose daily work makes the production possible. I am especially thankful to Lauren L. Murphy, Managing Editor, and Justin Howell for their work in copyediting, Colleen Stiller, Production Manager, Stephanie Nix, Production Assistant, and Tara Durheim, Associate Publisher for Academic and Monastic Markets.

Author's Introduction

"For These Things I Weep"
(Lam 1:16a)

The Babylonian invasion and destruction of Jerusalem and its temple are well documented in the historical book of 2 Kings 24:8–25:21 and in an account in 2 Chronicles 36:5-21. Details of the siege have also been added by the biblical prophet Jeremiah (39:1-10) and even portrayed by the prophetic actions of Ezekiel (4:1-17), both of whom experienced these events. The book of Lamentations renders its own account of this devastation and its aftermath. Unlike previous accounts, however, Lamentations narrates this catastrophe neither by rehearsing the historical details of captured royal officials nor by relating which professionals were carried into exile or by offering a tally of the valuable items ransacked from the temple before its fiery destruction. The historical specificity that would identify dates, important persons, or even Babylon itself as the archenemy responsible for the destruction is glaringly absent from these poems. Instead, the poetry of Lamentations generates a different rendition. It registers and witnesses to this monumental disaster through the cries and emotional outpourings of those on the ground. The chaotic and confused sentiments of actual people struggling to survive impregnate these verses. Amid the surrounding upheaval, siege, and subsequent famine, the true rawness of human suffering is etched in these poems and gives witness to the depths of human anguish. Both the cost of physical misery and the internal struggle resound in a choir of individual and communal voices echoing their efforts to endure. Bitter memories, theological crises, psychological confusion, and rock-bottom hopelessness saturate these poetic stanzas. Across Lamentations, candid human testimony memorializes this disastrous tragedy. As Francis Landy notes, Lamentations "marks with untampered immediacy, the focal calamity of the Bible, the destruction of Jerusalem in 586 BCE."[1]

Yet the lack of historical specificity in Lamentations allows for a timelessness regarding the suffering it makes audible. Its vivid images speak beyond the events that prompted the composition of these laments. It externalizes the internal complexities of the suffering, victimization, and tribulations that have, regrettably, continued to unfold through human history.

Still, there is more to lament here than even the vastness of human loss or the calamity of timeless warfare etched in the poetics of this book. In Lamentations, the multiple voices that narrate unspeakable suffering and labor to make sense of the surrounding horror do so at women's expense. Thus, women are well advised to exercise caution as they open this book. For the negative portrait of women in Lamentations as well as their implied suffering and degradation summon further lament because of this book.

As Lamentations opens, an overarching metaphor that receives extended elaboration in Lamentations 1 and 2 personifies Jerusalem as a woman. The first poem begins with woman Jerusalem (referred throughout this work as "Woman Zion") sketched as a grieving widow (Lam 1:1-2). She has lost a husband, as well as all that is implied as a result of that loss in a patriarchal society. She lacks protection, economic support, and social identity. Immediately, bereavement, aloneness, and pity define Woman Zion. As the poem unfolds, however, so too does the metaphoric portrait of Jerusalem. This widow is further defined by the loss of her children who have been taken away (Lam 1:5d). Hence, she also registers as an abandoned mother. Her children are carried off by the enemy because she is unable to protect them (1:5). Consequently, her status as tragic victim shifts. She begins to be assigned responsibility for

---

1. Francis Landy, "Lamentations," in *The Literary Guide to the Bible*, ed. Robert Alter and Frank Kermode (Cambridge: The Belknap Press, 1987), 329, quoted in Adele Berlin, *Lamentations* (Louisville: Westminster John Knox, 2002), 1.

the calamity that has befallen her children, who symbolize the inhabitants of the city. By the fifth verse of the first poem, no question remains as to culpability for the unfolding catastrophe. Blame for the destruction of Jerusalem, yet to be narrated, is laid squarely upon Woman Zion. "The LORD has made her suffer for the multitude of her transgressions" (Lam 1:5c).

Now the metaphorical woman becomes more than a grieving widow or incapable mother. A backstory is crafted that rehearses her iniquity, stemming from a time when she was an unfaithful wife who had taken lovers (1:8-9). Infidelity, shame, and immorality complicate Woman Zion's portrait and function as explanation for the city's destruction. As a follow-up, a narrative of her rape, assault, and abandonment (1:10)—which borders on pornographic—thickens her metaphoric description. These degrading assertions bolster the mounting sentiments regarding her culpability. Lamentably, such elaborations reinforce enduring notions that women somehow bring this type of punishment on themselves and, as a result, deserve the kind of violence that Woman Zion/Jerusalem incurs.

Though this highly charged sexual imagery remains confined to Lamentations 1 and 2, there are enduring consequences. The lamentable portrait of Woman Zion in the opening of the book supplies the only image for readers, which is likely summoned in their imaginations each time Jerusalem or Zion is referenced throughout the text. Subtly, each reference to her prompts recall of the initial metaphoric presence of the iniquitous city woman who bears responsibility for all the suffering therein. For women, however, there is yet more to lament than the persistence of this demeaning metaphor. Actual women register as frequent victims of the destruction recorded here and are painted as central figures in some of the most explicit images of suffering in these poems.

As Lamentations discloses the destruction's record of victims, women's anguish is portrayed alongside that of men. Young girls and boys are carried off into captivity by enemy troops. Exposition regarding war practices suggests these young women likely suffered particular trauma, often in the form of sexual violation. Additionally, women—like men—are slaughtered without mercy (2:21), but given women's role in the domestic sphere, their deaths leave children behind, presumably abandoned. Women who survive in the city are described as mothers who become widows. Thus, the loss of much more than husbands, killed or taken in warfare, befalls them. Within the confines of Zion, women are raped (5:11), likely by enemy forces that have overtaken the urban center. As the siege continues, famine wreaks havoc in the city. Now the depiction of women in their role as mothers serves as exponent of just how severe conditions have become. These mothers are not only unable to feed their starving children who are begging for food but also portrayed as caressing their dying infants against their dried-up breasts where these innocent ones should have been nourished. In the most graphic image of human travail, women's role shifts from that of victim to victimizer. As the siege continues and hunger grows more intense, the poetic verses disclose that compassionate mothers resort to boiling and eating their children. Here, the actions of women serve to narrate the utter loss of humanity prompted by this ongoing catastrophe. Mothers who have lost their maternal instinct symbolize the depravity that has warped the most elemental of relationships.

Jewish scholar Naomi Seidman has good reason to charge that Lamentations, because of its utter debasement of women, deserves to be excised from the canon.[2] Deryn Guest also argues that the negative power of the presiding metaphor is so detrimental for women that such texts warrant elimination from the tradition.[3] Indeed, the victimization of women portrayed here, as well as the depiction of Jerusalem as an immoral woman who gets what she deserves, are reprehensible. Lamentations portrays women as victims—victims of patriarchal society, of war, of a theological tradition, and of authors. Still, we have reason to claim this book as part of our religious heritage. Down through the ages, the representations of the Holocaust have been exhaustive. Whether in novels, paintings, movies, or plays, these various depictions have served as painful but necessary reminders of the inhumanity of which we humans are capable and the kinds of human mistreatment that must never happen again.[4] In a similar way, the preservation of this book gives notice of the biases, divisiveness, and misogynist attitudes regarding women, which even religious tradition is capable of promoting and which must be steadfastly resisted.

---

2. Naomi Seidman, "Burning the Book of Lamentations," in *Out of the Garden: Women Writers on the Bible*, ed. C. Buchmann and C. Spiegel (New York: Fawcett Columbine, 1992), 283.

3. Deryn Guest, "Hiding Behind the Naked Women in Lamentations: A Recriminative Response," *BibInt* 7 (1999): 413–48, at 444.

4. Kathleen M. O'Connor makes a similar observation regarding the library of testimony about the Holocaust and how "such truth telling becomes an act of survival"; see Kathleen M. O'Connor, *Lamentations and the Tears of the World* (Maryknoll, NY: Orbis Books, 2002), 5.

Yet, further justifications exist for claiming this book. Feminist interpretation of biblical texts not only exercises its prerogative by documenting the case against women, a prerogative already well exercised when it comes to Lamentations,[5] but also seeks to identify sources of strength and portraits of courageous resistance amid the rubble of misogynist landscapes. Hence, the interpretation that follows not only indicts the tradition for further victimizing women but also offers women who have been victimized or abused an occasion to join their voices with those of women who have gone before them. While it will offer unsettling glimpses of women's pain and suffering during the exile, it will also present Woman Zion as a courageous female voice who rises up from her victimization and boldly confronts an insolvent theology and its deity with the injustice of innocent suffering.

Literary Character

While the destruction of Jerusalem and the ensuing consequences for its inhabitants remain the focus of all five chapters, each poem exists as a self-contained composition offering a unique perspective on these events.[6] Lamentations 1 fixes on Jerusalem in the immediate aftermath of the destruction. It narrates the grief, shame, and desolation now surrounding the once-glorious city. Lamentations 2 recounts the physical decimation as an act of divine rage. As God's anger is unleashed on the city, the chapter concludes with Woman Zion's anger unleashed toward God. Lamentations 3, often thought of as the centerpiece of the book, drafts in detail the tribulations of exile. This poem offers, according to some interpretations, the only glimpse of hope in the whole book, though it quickly fades by the chapter's end. Lamentations 4 chronicles the ongoing consequences of the siege and then paints some of the most graphic pictures of the resulting suffering and human degradation. Finally, Lamentations 5 fashions the community's prayer of petition to

---

5. See, for example, Carleen R. Mandolfo, *Daughter Zion Talks Back to the Prophets: A Dialogic Theology of the Book of Lamentations*, SemeiaSt 58 (Atlanta: SBL Press, 2007); Mark J. Boda, Carol Dempsey, and LeAnn Snow Flesher, eds., *Daughter Zion: Her Portrait, Her Response* (Atlanta: SBL Press, 2012); F. W. Dobbs-Allsopp and Tod Linafelt, "The Rape of Zion in Thr 1, 10," *ZAW* 113 (2001): 77–81; Guest, "Hiding Behind the Naked Women," 413–48.

6. For characterization of each chapter not only with a distinctive perspective but also with a distinctive tone, see also Berlin, *Lamentations*, 7.

God to restore the broken relationship. In a collective emotional appeal, the people of Jerusalem plead with the Lord to not turn away from them forever.

Despite being distinct in perspective, these five poems are united in form as each employs some variation of an acrostic structure to create an artistic bond between them. In an acrostic, each line or stanza begins with successive letters of the Hebrew alphabet, from א, *aleph* to ת, *taw*. Hence, the first word of each of the three-line stanzas in Lamentations 1 and 2 begins with a successive alphabetic Hebrew letter.[7] Lamentations 3 continues this pattern in a more intensified form with the same alphabetical format, but with each successive letter introducing all three lines of each stanza. Lamentations 4 unfolds across two-line stanzas, each introduced by the successive alphabetic letter. Finally, Lamentations 5 appears at first glance to abandon the acrostic pattern, but its structure of twenty-two stanzas maintains the number of letters of the Hebrew alphabet. Thus, this final chapter indeed subtly participates in the artistry that unites the five poems.

Many scholars have noted that the acrostic pattern provides structural unity and coherence across these five chapters. The alphabetic framework establishes clear beginnings and endings that both separate the pieces but also join them together as belonging to one work. In its predictability, the acrostic form also helps to manage the unpredictable and precarious content narrated in these poems. It acts as a stabilizing force amid the disquiet and confusion of the suffering and loss made audible in the book. It provides order for the narrative of a world that seems out of control. The familiarity and successive order of its tight framework buffer the opposing ideas and contradictory sentiments that ricochet throughout these poems. Finally, predominance of the acrostic artistry suggests the intentionality with which these poems were fashioned. Nothing haphazard resides here. These carefully composed pieces, with their familiar frameworks, appear crafted to accommodate the complexity of suffering and the narrative of survival that unfold within. Still, such artistic intentionality by authors in a patriarchal context requires scrutiny in the hands of feminists. Leonard Shlain argues that the development of the alphabet caused a major shift in culture whereby the written word was

---

7. The order of the Hebrew letters פ, *pe*, and ע, *'ayin*, in chapters 2, 3, and 4 are reversed. Adele Berlin notes that this reversal "reflects an alternative order of the alphabet, also found in inscriptions dating from several centuries before 586 BCE at Kuntillet 'Ajrud and 'Izbet Sartah'" (ibid., 4).

favored over images.[8] "Whenever a culture elevates the written word at the expense of the image, patriarchy dominates. When the importance of the image supersedes the written word, feminine values and egalitarianism flourish."[9] Shlain ties the rise of linear rationality of the alphabetic to developing modes of comprehending reality that were masculine in character. These evolving capacities in turn functioned to suppress goddess worship in ancient Israel. Hence, this shift could indicate that the degradation and rejection of Woman Zion cohere with the excess of containment in the alphabetic acrostic poems of Lamentations. Further, Hugh Pyper notes that the transition from images to the written word "is at least suggestive that the repudiation of Zion is contained in so explicitly alphabetic a text, and that this structure is at its tightest in the third chapter, which most explicitly speaks in a male voice and looks to the male God."[10] Hence, while the predominance of the acrostic may serve to contain the chaotic content narrated in these poems, it may also work to constrain and obscure the feminine dimensions of the deity.

The book of Lamentations manifests elements of several different genres. A cry for help that opens Lamentations 1, 2, and 4, the call to mourn, the declaration of death, and the accompanying expressions of grief and bewilderment characteristic of the funeral dirge craft various contours of these poems. Features of the traditional lament, well documented in the biblical tradition, also permeate all of the chapters. The lament's characteristic complaint against enemies, circumstances, or even God, as well as the requisite cry for help, declaration of guilt, and petition for revenge against foes infuse these poems with the form and sentiment that coincide with the lament psalms. Finally, aspects of the city lament well documented in Sumerian texts also play a part in the composition of these five chapters.[11] The personification of Jerusalem as a woman, mother, and daughter in Lamentations 1 and 2 and a description of the ordeals and strife in Lamentations 3 and 4 manifest aspects of this particular form. That Lamentations features elements of several

8. Leonard Shlain, *The Alphabet Versus the Goddess: The Conflict between Word and Image* (New York: Penguin Books, 1999).

9. Ibid., 7.

10. Hugh S. Pyper, "Reading Lamentations," *JSOT* 95 (2001): 62–63. I am indebted to Pyper's work for directing me to Shlain's research and its importance for assessing the acrostic from a feminist perspective.

11. For a survey of research on the relationship of the city laments to Lamentations, see F. W. Dobbs-Allsopp, *Weep, O Daughter of Zion: A Study of the City-Lament Genre in the Hebrew Bible*, BibOr 44 (Rome: Pontifical Biblical Institute, 1993), 2–10.

genres enhances the rhetorical effectiveness derived from each. Rather than conforming to a rigid categorization of genre, Lamentations can be described as participating in a variety of genres in order to disclose the complexity of a whole community's experience of this focal calamity.[12]

Characteristic of biblical poetry, parallelism works to establish both connections and contrast between adjacent lines and stanzas. Repetition serves to emphasize themes. Poetic imagery points to the experiences that eclipse words. The question of meter remains a debated topic. Karl Budde titled the meter in Lamentations "*qinah*," from the Hebrew word for a lament. He noted that the *qinah* line was the dominant line in these poems, identified as a 3+2 rhythm existing primarily in Lamentations 1–4. In this format, the first stich of a line consists of three stresses. The second stich follows, consisting of just two stresses, as if "dying away in a lamenting fashion," as is characteristic of funeral dirges and death.[13] For example,

> He has made my flesh and my skin waste away,
> And [he has] broken my bones. (Lam 3:4)

Translations often obscure the *qinah* meter, and scholars since Budde suggest that *qinah* is one of several meter types that reside here.

As Lamentations resounds with the community's witness to the destruction of Jerusalem, it hosts a variety of voices that narrate individuals' experiences. All these speakers are creations of the literary pieces and are not to be confused with the poet(s) who composed these laments. In Lamentations 1 and 2, an unnamed individual reports the destruction with the dispassionate demeanor of an objective reporter. He will be called an observer. In the second chapter, however, the human suffering he describes unmasks his composure, and he begins to admit his own suffering and struggle. In these first two chapters, this observer interacts with another character, introduced as Daughter Zion (1:6). This second speaker, Jerusalem personified, speaks as a weeping widow and

---

12. With Miriam J. Bier, *'Perhaps There Is Hope': Reading Lamentations as a Polyphony of Pain, Penitence, and Protest*, LHBOTS (New York: Bloomsbury T&T Clark, 2015), 8, who—citing Carol A. Newsom, *The Book of Job: A Contest of Moral Imaginations* (Oxford: Oxford University Press, 2003), 12, and M. M. Bakhtin, *Problems of Dostoevsky's Poetics*, ed. and trans. Caryl Emerson (Minneapolis: University of Minnesota Press, 1984), 106—aptly summarizes that texts do not so much belong to genres but participate in, move in and out of, and invoke aspects of a variety of genres.

13. See Budde's contributions as cited in Delbert R. Hillers, *Lamentations*, AB 7A (Garden City, NY: Doubleday, 1992), xxxi.

mother, recounting the violence that has befallen both herself and her children. Dianne Bergant notes that characteristic of the patriarchal ethos in ancient Near Eastern societies, cities were often portrayed as women whose fertile terrain was protected by men. Literature described these ancient cities as mothers who enclosed their inhabitants in their walls to protect them,[14] but, as we shall see, a cultural understanding that portrays cities as mothers and the inhabitants as her children can have fatal consequences for women in a patriarchal setting.

Woman Zion does speak in these poems. Twice she responds to the observer in Lamentations 1 and has the last words in Lamentations 2. Thereafter, she is not heard from directly, though reference is still made to her. In Lamentations 3, a new voice is introduced, identified only as the "strong man."[15] He represents the noble male resident who might be assumed to rescue people from the aftermath of the havoc. Instead, he himself succumbs to the calamity and also speaks for the community with whom he suffers. In Lamentations 4, another observer steps into the limelight. Whether this reporting voice is the same voice heard in Lamentations 1 and 2 is not clear. This later observer's disposition seems distinct, and he sounds much more embroiled in the crisis along with the community who also speaks with him. Finally, Lamentations 5 belongs to the collective voice of the community. They are the denigrated and impoverished Judean remnant who have lost their king, their temple, and all that defined them as God's people.

Interspersed among these key speakers across the chapters are other voices. For example, onlookers who pass by Woman Zion utter mockery and degrading comments toward her. Enemies of the city are quoted as they deride the city and its inhabitants. Children starving in the streets are heard crying out to their mothers for food, and an occasional chorus of onlookers, peoples, and nations cries out against Woman Zion, charging her as guilty. Hence, these laments harbor a multitude of voices both within and outside the community, granting a wide view of the destruction of the city and the harrowing aftermath.

Throughout the entire book of Lamentations, the divine voice is glaringly absent. Though God is beseeched on several occasions, nowhere does the Lord respond. Amid all the voices narrating human suffering

---

14. Dianne Bergant, *Lamentations*, AOTC (Nashville: Abingdon, 2003), 15–16.

15. The NRSV translation used throughout this study does not carry the translation of the Hebrew גבר "strong man" but renders it "I am the one" (3:1). "Strong man," however, will be used here to better convey the character of this speaker.

and the various perspectives on the destruction of Jerusalem echoing in these poems, God remains utterly silent.

Authorship

A long history of tradition has ascribed the book of Lamentations to the prophet Jeremiah. The practice likely stemmed from the Septuagint, the oldest Greek version of the Old Testament, in which the book of Lamentations opens by identifying the work with this prophet. "And it came to pass after Israel had gone in captivity, and Jerusalem was laid waste, that Jeremiah sat weeping and composed this lament over Jerusalem and said . . ." (Lam 1:1 LXX). An even earlier text in Chronicles also points to Jeremiah as the likely author. "Jeremiah also uttered a lament for Josiah, and all the singing men and singing women have spoken of Josiah in their laments to this day. They made these a custom in Israel; they are recorded in the Laments" (2 Chr 35:25). Though the Chronicler is not specific in assigning the laments in the book of Lamentations to the prophet, the citation has encouraged the tradition of the prophet's authorship. The references to the destruction of Jerusalem in 587 BCE do argue for a composition date around the time of the prophet's activity. In addition, the book of Jeremiah itself includes frequent lamentations in anticipation of the destruction.

Many irreconcilable differences in style and content between the books of Jeremiah and Lamentations, however, have been noted. Claus Westermann's summary that the assignment of Lamentations to Jeremiah "has for all intents and purposes been abandoned" summarizes the current scholarly opinion on the matter,[16] and while the five poems within Lamentations are united by their acrostic form, most likely they emerged from several authors. The familiar practice of enlisting women as trained professional mourners (Jer 9:17-20; 2 Sam 1:24; Ezek 32:16-18) opens up the possibility that women may have had a role in their composition or in the circulation of these five laments among the community.[17] Moreover, the Masoretic text makes no reference to Jeremiah's authorship. Unlike its placement in the Christian Old Testament, Lamentations in the

16. Claus Westermann, *Lamentations: Issues and Interpretation*, trans. Charles Muenchow (Minneapolis: Fortress, 1994), 58.

17. Kathleen M. O'Connor, "Lamentations," in *Women's Bible Commentary*, ed. Carol A. Newsom, Sharon H. Ringe, and Jacqueline E. Lapsley, 3rd ed. (Louisville: Westminster John Knox, 2012), 278.

Jewish canon resides among the Megilloth (Festival scrolls), confirming a long tradition of their liturgical use for the community. Today, Jews continue to recite Lamentations on the ninth of Ab, remembering the two destructions of the temple—first in 587 BCE by the Babylonians and then in 60 CE by the Romans. Furthermore, because of their lack of historical specificity, these laments have a timelessness that enables them to have relevance throughout Jewish history up to the Holocaust. The recitation of portions of Lamentations by some Christian communities each year during their Holy Week liturgies testifies further to their enduring relevance.

Lamentations 1

"Is There Any Sorrow Like My Sorrow . . ."

The Power of a Metaphor

One of the ways feminist readers and interpreters deal with the biblical texts is by documenting the case against women that we find there. Unwilling to risk complicity with the violence too often encountered in these religious traditions, feminists have refused to read past or accommodate either the overt or covert instances of violence against women. Lamentations 1 poses an especial challenge for women readers. The images of violence in regard to women are particularly vivid and difficult here. In this opening poem as well as in Lamentations 2, Zion—metaphorically characterized as a desolate woman—presides as subject of the lament, but though she functions as the central focus of the poem, her portrait is deeply lamentable. Not until the second half of the chapter (Lam 1:12-22) do we actually hear her voice. First, we must endure the report of a male observer in whose account she is objectified.

The argument that the image of Zion as a violated woman functions only as metaphor does not appreciate the power of this literary device. Metaphors originate in social contexts and often reinforce elements of a certain social milieu. They participate in the web of socio-historical, cultural, and religious constructions of such settings. Moreover, metaphors gain meaning because they function within a cultural framework in conjunction with the established rules, customs, and understandings.[1] At the same time, cultural frameworks bolster the kinship between the two elements of the metaphor. Thus, as this first lament unfolds, the two components of the metaphor—an abandoned, abused woman and the decimated city that she represents—move back and forth across the verses. The portrait of the devastated city and that of an abused punished woman become so closely aligned that gradually the images fuse. In the process, not only does the pitiful portrait of the violated woman grant a glance at the ruinous remains of Jerusalem, but the grim portrait of the punished city encourages the stereotype of woman as violated victim who invites the abuse that comes her way. "It is now generally understood that far from being merely decorative, metaphors have real cognitive content."[2] They encourage hearers to participate in the development and maintenance of the metaphor's meanings. Thus, such images not only reinforce elements of a social context but can become etched in both the culture and the consciousness of participating readers down through the ages.[3] As a result, the consequences of making normative the notion of an abused, desolate woman who gets what she deserves are legion and hardly need to be detailed.

Lament Structure

Like the other four chapters that follow, the acrostic format stylizes this opening poem where each three-line strophe (with the exception of v. 7) begins with a successive letter of the Hebrew alphabet. Some would argue that this carefully planned format brings order to the chaos narrated within. Kathleen O'Connor takes this idea a step further, suggesting that the alphabetic devices "embody struggles of survivors to

---

1. See Renita Weems, *Battered Love: Marriage, Sex, and Violence in the Hebrew Prophets* (Minneapolis: Fortress, 1995), 12–24, for a discussion on the metaphoric images of battered violated women across the prophetic tradition that normalizes and reinforces such a cultural template as common and acceptable.

2. Carol A. Newsom, "A Maker of Metaphors: Ezekiel's Oracles against Tyre," in *Interpreting the Prophets*, ed. James L. Mays and Paul J. Actemeier (Philadelphia: Fortress, 1987), 189.

3. See George Lakoff and Mark Turner, *More Than Cool Reason: A Field Guide to Poetic Metaphor* (Chicago: University of Chicago Press, 1989), for an extensive discussion of the social dynamics accompanying working metaphors.

contain and control the chaos of unstructured pain."[4] Feminist readers, however, might also note and beware that the very widely recognized and accepted acrostic organization in form could also subtly formalize and endorse as acceptable the cultural image therein—that of a ravaged, abandoned woman.

The elements of this first poem conform to the laments that are frequently encountered in the biblical tradition. Characteristic of this genre, these recitations typically include attention to the nature of the suffering, the cause of the suffering, those who aggravate or are responsible for the suffering, and a plea to God to resolve the pain being endured, but the poem in Lamentations 1 differs from the characteristic lament format in that it does not end on a note of hope or confidence that the outcry has been heard. Though Woman Zion does appeal to God, she gives no hint that her plea has been received. In fact, throughout this chapter and throughout the entire book of Lamentations, there is no divine response. God, if even in earshot of these recitations, remains utterly silent.

Two Voices Interact

Two speeches of almost equal length structure the poem, providing two takes on the suffering of Woman Zion—one observed (1:1-11) and one experienced (1:12-22). The first speaker presents dispassionately, as if hired as a professional reporter documenting the suffering of Woman Zion with coolly detached description. Thus, he will be referred to as the "observer." At first glance, Woman Zion is the subject about whom he reports. Yet his impartial, emotionless description objectifies her. Moreover, when his account moves beyond what is publicly observable to what constitutes sexual violations and even rape, his reporting provides details that suggest his stance as voyeuristic. While his third-person speech implies that he is the only one making these observations, he also observes others witnessing the horror and shame visited upon Woman Zion. He notes that her pursuers (1:3c), passersby (1:12), and former friends (1:2c) all stand by. He has a quality of all-knowingness embedded in his rhetoric. When he narrates the details of her depraved condition, his persistent use of the adjective "all" (כל) in his descriptions suggests the comprehensive nature of that which she has lost and those who have turned against her (1:2b, c, 3a, 6a, 7b, 10b, 11a). Chronicling

---

4. Kathleen M. O'Connor, *Lamentations and the Tears of the World* (Maryknoll, NY: Orbis Books, 2002), 12.

her suffering with such hyperbole reinforces the totality and completeness of the injury surrounding Woman Zion. Nothing in the observer's poetic narrative appears unplanned here. The first half of his oration describes Woman Zion as desolate and defiled (1:1-5), and the second half of his account offers explanation for her sorry state (1:5b-11). Only toward the end of his speech do readers realize that Woman Zion is in fact on the sidelines, hearing this detailed witness of her travail. Briefly she interrupts him (1:9c). However, she does not offer rebuttal or refute his testimony. Rather, she makes what sounds like a spontaneous and desperate outcry to God: "O Lord, look at my affliction, for the enemy has triumphed!" (1:9c). She seeks rescue (1:9c) not only from her shattered life but also perhaps from the observer's seething report as well as the indicting gaze of those witnessing her pitiful state.

When Woman Zion's speech finally begins in the second half of the poem (1:11c-22), her first-person account claims the suffering and desolation from the subjective position of her own experience. The external details of the observer's account in the first half of the poem are now saturated with evidence of her interior pain. Readers have access here to her gut-wrenching anguish that threatens to rupture the very fibers of her being. Comprehensive loss, excessive personal violation, public humiliation, and failure to understand why prompt Woman Zion's oration, but the frequent iteration that "there is no one to comfort her" (1:2, 7, 9, 16, 17, 21) in combination with God's silence leave her even more vulnerable and exposed than her own words suggest. When the observer interrupts her speech in verse 17, he too notes her aloneness and deserted state. As one scholar astutely observes, Woman Zion's passionate narration testifies to the "moral authority of her status as a survivor."[5] Still, it should not be missed that Woman Zion's firsthand report witnesses to the gravity and depth of her pain alongside her prevailing awareness that there is no one to comfort her.

The Observer's Account (Lam 1:1-11)

The observer's report commences with the particle "How" (איכה). This initial exclamation serves a dual purpose. It opens the poem with a question that wonders how this destruction could have happened (1:1a). It also stands alone—"How?"—as expression of the incredulity

---

5. Ibid., 18.

1:1How lonely sits the city
    that once was full of people!
How like a widow she has become,
    she that was great among the
      nations!
She that was a princess among
    the provinces
    has become a vassal.

2She weeps bitterly in the night,
    with tears on her cheeks;
among all her lovers
    she has no one to comfort her;
all her friends have dealt
    treacherously with her,

they have become her
    enemies.

3Judah has gone into exile with
    suffering
and hard servitude;
she lives now among the nations,
    and finds no resting place;
her pursuers have all overtaken
    her
    in the midst of her distress.

4The roads to Zion mourn,
    for no one comes to the
      festivals;

and gasped horror of that which he observes and subsequently details. Employing the metaphor of a violated, guilt-ridden woman blamed for the atrocities that have befallen her children, he describes the suffering of Zion/Judah.

Goddesses were frequently identified with cities in the ancient Near East. Gradually they become absorbed into the city identity itself as these female deities are supplanted and replaced by male deities.[6] As a result, the female characterization of a city became a well-documented ancient practice.[7] Ancient cities were walled to protect their citizens, giving rise to the image of the inhabitants as children encircled and made safe by a mother's surrounding wall of care. Moreover, maternal fertility was celebrated, as it ensured that cites would continue and flourish. But here, Zion is anything but a royal mother protecting her children. Instead, the once-honored mother has become a vulnerable widow, a deplorable sinner, an abused woman, and a rape victim. Thus, the observer assumes the maternal city-woman image to launch his chronicle of her reversal of fortune. Across this opening description, he details three major shifts in the portrait of Woman Zion.

6. See the in-depth discussion of these transitions in Tikva Frymer Kensky, *In the Wake of the Goddesses: Women, Culture, and the Biblical Transformation of Pagan Myth* (New York: Ballentine Books, 1993), 70–83.
7. Dianne Bergant, *Lamentations*, AOTC (Nashville: Abingdon, 2003), 27–28.

all her gates are desolate,
    her priests groan;
her young girls grieve,
    and her lot is bitter.

⁵Her foes have become the
        masters,
    her enemies prosper,
because the Lᴏʀᴅ has made her
        suffer
    for the multitude of her
        transgressions;
her children have gone away,
    captives before the foe.

⁶From daughter Zion has departed
    all her majesty.

Her princes have become like
        stags
    that find no pasture;
they fled without strength
    before the pursuer.

⁷Jerusalem remembers,
    in the days of her affliction and
        wandering
all the precious things
    that were hers in days of old.
When her people fell into the hand
        of the foe,
    and there was no one to help her,
the foe looked on mocking
    over her downfall.

Three Shifts in Portraying Woman Zion

First, the change in her circumstances emerges as stark and staggering. Portrayed as once a princess among the provinces (1:1d), Woman Zion assumes a new demoted status as a vassal. The satisfaction once derived from her greatness among the nations (1:1c) is replaced with inconsolable grief and tears she now weeps (1:2a). The people that gave fullness and meaning to her existence are gone. Roads are empty, her gates are desolate, and all signs of pilgrims have disappeared. The opening line of verse 1 summarizes the consequences of these changed circumstances: "How lonely sits the city." Once surrounded with people, she now resides alone, abandoned, and lacking any human solidarity.

Such isolation suggests the second shift—a devastating change in relationships. Her new status as widow (1:1) immediately bespeaks a loss of social connectedness. It also suggests her vulnerability in a society before which she has lost all social standing and definition. Those who once honored her now despise her (1:8b). That her inhabitants have been taken into captivity indicates further that she has been cut off from those who made up her social network. Those she knew as friends have become enemies. Moreover, the observer reports that these enemies are now her masters (1:5a) as well as agents of her downfall. Finally, her children, those whom she cared most about and who gave meaning and definition to her life, "have gone away, captives before the foe" (1:5d).

[8]Jerusalem sinned grievously,
so she has become a
mockery;
all who honored her despise her,
for they have seen her
nakedness;
she herself groans,
and turns her face away.

[9]Her uncleanness was in her
skirts;
she took no thought of her
future;
her downfall was appalling,
with none to comfort her.
"O LORD, look at my affliction,

for the enemy has triumphed!"

[10]Enemies have stretched out
their hands
over all her precious things;
she has even seen the nations
invade her sanctuary,
those whom you forbade
to enter your congregation.

[11]All her people groan
as they search for bread;
they trade their treasures for food
to revive their strength.
Look, O LORD, and see
how worthless I have become.

The disquieting shift in circumstances and the dramatic change in relationships necessarily bring about a change in identity and a change in self-understanding for Woman Zion. In the first verse of the poem, the observer highlights this drastic about-face. She who was a noble princess has become a vassal, best understood as a day laborer.[8] She weeps bitterly, inconsolably. The image of her "in the night" suggests she is alone in this grief (1:2a). Across verses 2-5, a litany of those who oppose her defines and magnifies her isolation. The friends turned foes (1:2c, d), the unidentified pursuers (1:3c), and the enemies who will act against her (1:5a) craft a vivid image of her isolation and assault. Then the observer immediately connects this tally of affliction directly to the Lord's intent to make her suffer. Finally, the observer, perhaps perplexed by the scope and gravity of the suffering all around, settles on an explanation. He connects the divine response to an underlying cause to explain her anguish. "The LORD has made her suffer for the multitude of her transgressions" (1:5b, c). Zion is suffering because she has sinned.

In light of this indictment, the afflictions of all those affected by the destruction are now tied to Woman's Zion's transgressions. The pain and anguish of her children (1:5d), the young girls (1:4d), the priests

8. Adele Berlin, *Lamentations* (Louisville: Westminster John Knox, 2002), 49, notes that vassals bond to conquerors were required to provide collateral or services, hence the notion of a "day laborer" in Jerusalem's case is apt.

(1:4c), the past residents of the city (1:4b), and even the princes portrayed as stags that now are without provisions (1:6b) stem from the guilt of Woman Zion. "All the precious things that were hers in days of old" (1:7b) paint a painful contrast with the losses and afflictions of her people in the present. Though once chosen for a covenantal relationship with God, the now pitiful Woman Zion bears the evidence of her infidelity and sinfulness. Indicted for "her multitude of transgressions," she is punished by God. Here she is not only judged as guilty. She herself bears responsibility for her own immense suffering, which is defined by the suffering of others. As if struggling to account for the incomprehensible devastation that now characterizes Woman Zion, the observer reiterates emphatically, "Jerusalem sinned grievously" (1:8a).

Sexual Inuendos Hasten an Indictment

In verses 8b-9c, the observer's report becomes particularly intimate and detailed, as if the newly public nature of Woman Zion's guilt grants him license. The observer enlists language thick with sexual connotation. In verse 8, נידה (*nidah*; "mockery"), a word occurring only here in the biblical tradition, could refer to menstrual impurity by means of a play on words. The Hebrew word נדה (*niddah*), which occurs in verse 17, carries a general meaning of impurity often associated with menstruation. The mention of her nakedness (1:8) and uncleanness in her skirts (1:9) in the following lines encourages hearing נדה (*niddah*; "impurity") as the intended reference. The Hebrew root from which נידה derives can also be interpreted as "a shaking of the head in mockery," which coincides with the previous image of the foe looking on in mockery at her downfall in verse 7.[9] Finally, some defend a meaning of נידה as "homeless or aimless," with reference to Zion that echoes her days of wandering, as cited earlier (1:7a).[10]

Reference to "her nakedness" (1:8) occasions frequent associations with forbidden sexual activity (Lev 18:7-19; 20:17-18; Ezek 16:36-37; 23:10, 18) and is thus a particularly damning indictment. Such nakedness is also associated with shame (Isa 47:3; Nah 3:5) and thus accounts for the

9. See Miriam J. Bier, *'Perhaps There Is Hope': Reading Lamentations as a Polyphony of Pain, Penitence, and Protest*, LHBOTS (New York: Bloomsbury T&T Clark, 2015), 50, who cites HALOT 696, and offers a discussion of the three possible meanings of *nidah* in this instance.

10. Berlin, *Lamentations*, 53–54.

descriptions of the mockery directed at Woman Zion (Lam 1:7b, 8a), but the text is not clear as to what caused this exposure. Despite the utter lack of any mention of specific sin thus far, the assumption of sexual immorality is still readily made in interpretations.[11] Coupled with the obscure reference (נידה) to Woman Zion's impurity, some kind of sexual immorality is often readily assumed. Her indictment as adulterer receives further endorsement by the upcoming mention of the uncleanness of her skirts (1:9a).

For many commentators, the uncleanness in her skirts bears a strong suggestion of wanton sexual behavior. Some readily take this to mean she has participated in forbidden sexual encounters.[12] Others understand the uncleanness as reference to the stain of menstruation here. "The metaphorical nature of the imagery, and the possible origin of the people's sin in idolatry and defiling the land with blood (Ezra 9:11), suggest the ritual uncleanness of menstruation could be a further metaphor for the moral impurity of blood that defiles the land."[13] Berlin, however, rejects such arguments and makes clear that menstruation is not a sin. The impurity here results from her sexual immorality: "She is a whore."[14]

As the sexual innuendos amass across verses 8b-9c, they indict Woman Zion and reinforce the pronouncement of her pervasive sinfulness (Lam 1:5). In addition, they encourage interpreters to reread earlier references to her suffering as indications of her sinful way of life. The loss of her "lovers" (1:2b), "her pursuers overtaking her in her narrow straits" (1:3d),[15] "her friends dealing treacherously with her" (1:2c), and the memory of "all the precious things that were hers" (1:7b) previously conjured pity but now evoke revulsion. Bier observes that reference to Jerusalem's "precious things" (1:7b) may well intend sexual connotations, suggesting her genitals, given the previous references to "her lovers" (1:2) and those foes who have become "masters" over her (1:5a).[16] Though the text never

---

11. Christopher Wright, *The Message of Lamentations* (Downers Grove, IL: InterVarsity Press, 2015), 64; Robert B. Salters, *Lamentations: A Critical and Exegetical Commentary*, ICC (New York: T&T Clark, 1994), 61; Tremper Longman III, *Jeremiah, Lamentations*, NIBC (Peabody, MA: Hendrickson, 2008), 346–47; Delbert R. Hillers, *Lamentations*, AB 7A (Garden City, NY: Doubleday, 1992), 23–24.

12. Berlin, *Lamentations*, 65.

13. Bier, *'Perhaps There Is Hope,'* 52.

14. Berlin, *Lamentations*, 55.

15. Reading with the Hebrew here as the sexual innuendo is obscured in the NRSV translation.

16. Bier, *'Perhaps There Is Hope,'* 51.

narrates Zion as an adulterer, there is a great deal of confluence among readers leading to this conclusion. Even though the case for such sexual impropriety is based on ambiguous references in the text, the dominant interpretations forward certainty. "This apparently pitiful woman had taken lovers, she acted immorally, and she deserved her punishment."[17]

All too often, women avoid reporting sexual assault. Guilt, fear of being blamed, shame, and the tragically frequent experience of not being believed number among the reasons given by these victims. Hence, rape and the resulting victimization are crimes that frequently go unrecognized and thus unpunished. If reported, the woman is often blamed and thus further victimized. That only textual inferences indict Woman Zion as an adulterer and that these references cultivate ambiguity rather than certainty warrant suspicion. Her nakedness may be the product of exposing herself to lovers or being shamed for engaging in sexual impropriety. Her nakedness, however, could also be the result of sexual assault or a violent crime against her. In wartime, a conquering enemy often humiliated captives by stripping them of their garments and displaying their nakedness. Bergant notes the surprising similarity of Isaiah 47:1-3, in which "the prophet mocks virgin daughter Babylon predicting that her nakedness will be uncovered and her shame will be seen."[18] That Woman Zion responds to the exposure of her nakedness by groaning and turning her face away (1:8d) readily coincides with such degrading treatment.

The reference to uncleanness in her skirts (1:9a) could refer to blood that is not necessarily from menstruation. Instead, it could function as evidence of forced sexual intercourse.[19] Rape of female subjects was common wartime practice where men violated other men's property. As a result, these abused women became defiled objects of male hostility and their insatiable schemes of revenge. Given the shame of her uncovered nakedness and the trauma of sexual defilement, it makes sense that "she took no thought of her future" (1:9b). Such degradation and maltreatment leave one without hope for a future. While the ambiguity of the text allows for a presumption of adultery, it also occasions the real probability that assault and rape as punishment are being narrated here. Victim in the text and victim of interpretations, Woman Zion indeed suffers greatly.

---

17. Berlin, *Lamentations*, 49.

18. Bergant, *Lamentations*, 41.

19. Dobbs-Allsopp and Linafelt elaborate rape images in 1:10b-c, 12b, 13c, 22b to support the case for rape here as well. See F. W. Dobbs-Allsopp and Tod Linafelt, "The Rape of Zion in Thr 1, 10," *ZAW* 113 (2001): 77–81.

But surpassing all this anguish is an even more intolerable reality. There is "none to comfort her" (1:9c).

Woman Zion Redefines Her Affliction (Lam 1:9c)

Amid reports that raise suspicions about her guilt and the public descriptions of her punishments, Woman Zion can no longer keep quiet. For the first time, readers are made aware that she has been listening to the litany of accusations that serve to explain her pitiful state. In Lamentations 1:9c, Woman Zion interrupts the observer's catalog but does not speak to him. Instead, she cries to God for rescue. "O Lord, look at my affliction, for the enemy has triumphed!" (1:9c). Though object of the observer's derisive speech up to this point, she now becomes the speaking subject. Her prayer becomes her personal testimony. She makes no confession of any sin or guilt on her part. She does not turn to God seeking forgiveness. Instead, she defines the affliction and suffering she experiences as the result of her enemy's triumph. Readers and interpreters are quick to assume that she is referring to the nations that have overcome her and carried her into exile, but her collective enemy may also include those who have made her victim in their construal of history, as in the observer's report.

"She Gets What She Deserves"? (Lam 1:10-11)

As if to ignore her presence and silence her voice, the observer quickly interrupts Woman Zion's testimony (1:10-11b). He seems, however, not to be reporting to interested onlookers any longer but rather to be speaking directly to God. Though in a somewhat more sympathetic tone, he continues with a few even more violent details of her sorry state. "Enemies have stretched out their hands over all her precious things" (1:10) suggests sexual molestation. Invasion of her inner sanctuary by the nations (1:10) bespeaks rape. While no one would deny the imagery portending sexual assault here, some interpreters have been quick to read the rape images here retrospectively into the earlier language of verses 8b-9c, leading to the suggestion that "Zion's wanton behaviors have brought about the inevitable upon herself."[20] Such "blame the victim"

---

20. Alan Mintz, *Hurban: Responses to Catastrophe in Hebrew Literature* (New York: Columbia University Press, 1984), 25; and Charles William Miller, "Reading Voices: Personification, Dialogism, and the Reader of Lamentations 1," *BibInt* 9 (2001): 398–99.

sentiments unfortunately continue to echo in the lives of women today who suffer the violence of sexual assault. Still, as the observer earlier suggested, this is punishment for breach of covenant (1:5b), but such a theology not only charges the suffering, violated woman as bearing evidence of her guilt; it makes the mechanism of punishment a duplicate of the sinful deed itself. The sexual impropriety of adultery is punished by the sexual impropriety of rape. In the first instance, woman is indicted; in the second instance, no one is indicted. More significant, this kind of theology identifies God as abuser of Woman Zion.

From the Dublin Women's Prison

My name is "Mendoza" and I am in my early twenties. I used to try to look tough and act cool and I needed to appear as if I was always in control. But much inside of me is broken . . . really broken. I had a boyfriend who was abusive. He would hit me if I said the wrong thing or if I did not do things the way he wanted. He would force me to have sex with him whenever it pleased him. I could not have my own friends. He introduced me to drugs. One night we were both high. He started to hit me and then started to force himself on me. I repeatedly asked him to stop but every one of my cries was interrupted by the impact of his fist on my face. As he began to rape me, I grabbed a kitchen knife and stabbed him. He died. Our society has judged me a murderer and unworthy to live free in society. I guess I am unworthy because now I only feel ashamed, worthless, and broken.

Anonymous

Uncomforted, Unheard—Woman Zion Speaks (Lam 1:12-16)

When Woman Zion finally has the wherewithal to raise her voice, we are privy to her emotional turmoil and destitution. Pain permeates her utterances and suggests her delirious state. Moreover, her descriptions offer insight as to her subjective takes on two accounts—her own experience of suffering and her experience of God. First, her experience of suffering opens an invitation to witness her travail. The aloneness in which she is shrouded resounds in the desperation of her initial outcry. She summons anyone to acknowledge that her sorrow is beyond all imagining (1:12). Here she seems willing to call upon not only the observer, whose report she has had to endure, but also those bystanders whose mockery scorned

¹²Is it nothing to you, all you who
        pass by?
    Look and see
if there is any sorrow like my sorrow,
        which was brought upon me,
which the LORD inflicted
        on the day of his fierce anger.

¹³From on high he sent fire;
        it went deep into my bones;
he spread a net for my feet;
        he turned me back;
he has left me stunned,
        faint all day long.

¹⁴My transgressions were bound
        into a yoke;
        by his hand they were
                fastened together;
they weigh on my neck,

sapping my strength;
    the Lord handed me over
        to those whom I cannot
                withstand.

¹⁵The LORD has rejected
        all my warriors in the midst of
                me;
he proclaimed a time against me
        to crush my young men;
the Lord has trodden as in a wine
                press
        the virgin daughter Judah.

¹⁶For these things I weep;
        my eyes flow with tears;
for a comforter is far from me,
        one to revive my courage;
my children are desolate,
        for the enemy has prevailed.

her. She offers a litany of the pain erupting from within. She narrates her anguish as fire "deep into my bones" (1:13). She likens her pain to being trapped, her feet ensnared within a net (1:13b). The heaviness of such affliction weighs like a yoke about her neck (1:14). Such encumbrances leave her staggering, feeling faint, and utterly vanquished (1:13c). She senses herself crushed, trodden down like grapes in a wine press (1:15). Exacerbating the already intolerable gut-wrenching suffering, she herself now testifies to what the observer has already twice made clear (1:2, 9). In the midst of such suffering, there is no one to comfort her (1:16).

Amid Woman Zion's complete aloneness, God remains unresponsive. The Lord remains utterly silent. God not only is unresponsive to her pain and alienation but also has ordered this suffering. The One who controls history has not rescued her but in fact has caused her downfall. Instead of lifting her up from this anguish, God has prevailed against her. Her description of her experience of God is intertwined with the previous description of her experience of suffering. Like a warrior deity, God marks their encounter. Images from warfare permeate her description. God has hurled fire, as in military destructions of cities (1:13a), and spread a net, as when captives are encircled and contained (1:13b). The language of "bound into a yoke" and "fastened together" suggests the capture and imprisonment by those overcome in warfare (1:14a, b). As Woman Zion concludes this first round of subjective retellings, she reminds us that this is why she weeps and why her "eyes flow with tears" (1:16). "The enemy has prevailed" (1:16). Once again, the identity of "the enemy" remains unclear. She may be speaking of the hostile nations that have besieged the city, or she may be referencing her experience of God.

She Has No One to Comfort Her

Weeping Jerusalem, violated and abandoned, without possessions, hope, or comfort, eerily prefigures the centuries-long experiences in the United States of African slaves and their descendants. Our nation has subjected Africans and African Americans to captivity throughout four hundred years of slavery: Jim Crow oppression, legally enforced segregation, and now the bondage of systemic inequality. Those of European descent, like myself, rarely have the courage to listen to tales of unspeakable violence and oppression. Yet, we can read in Lamentations the suffering of people who have been brutally victimized to serve their captors' needs, with no comfort from any quarter, not even from God. Perhaps in reading Lamentations with an open mind and heart we can recognize ourselves in the passersby in Jerusalem and respond in a way that comforts.

How can we offer comfort? In a simple way, by listening we offer basic human dignity as comfort to people shattered and struggling. We can stop and listen. We cannot continue to pass by and ignore the injustices in our nation that black and brown people endure. We can pay attention with humility and respect to their experiences. In listening, we begin to understand how historic oppressions continue today in racist economic and social structures inflicting injury over and over again. In sharing the lament of people of color honestly and authentically, we claim the open wounds of violence as our community's wounds. In understanding our individual and collective responsibility for racial oppression in the United States, we create the possibility of a different future where justice and comfort might be the norm.

What comfort is there for people who experience racial violence and oppression? It is not my place to tell those wounded by racism what to think, feel, or do. Yet, to the extent that racism distorts our whole community, for wisdom we might look to those who have walked the twofold path of lament and resistance ahead of us. Preaching to all people of good will fifty years ago Martin Luther King addressed particularly people whose lives had been shattered by segregation and racism. He harshly condemned bitterness, isolation, fatalism, and resignation to the so-called will of God. His call is the same to victim, bystander, beneficiary, or victor: *Actively resist injustice and oppression.*

Contrary to the tragic observation in Lamentations, "She has no one to comfort her," there *is* comfort for those who experience captivity, violence, and oppression and those who witness it, whether in our nation or anywhere in the world. Comfort takes root as respect and validation in a neighbor's quiet presence or in public weeping and witness. Comfort then bears fruit in nonviolent resistance, saying no to persecution and domination. Finally, comfort grows in strength and potency in the faith that God accompanies humanity in the universe's journey to justice. So, let us set things right—lest it be said of our generation, "There was no one to comfort her."

Alison Benders

There Is No One to Comfort Her (Lam 1:17)

As if to correct the direction of Woman Zion's subjective account that is unfolding, the observer interrupts her and insists on a clarification. His opening image of Zion stretching out her hands (1:17a) recalls the image of enemies stretching out their hands (1:10a) in the process of sexually assaulting her. He reiterates not only that no one responds this time but that "there is no one to comfort her" (1:17a). He concurs with Woman Zion's assessment that the Lord has made the neighbors of Jacob its foes. He goes on, however, to qualify that this situation of hostility is the result of Jerusalem's iniquity. Woman Zion's immorality has led to her downfall. She has become "a filthy thing [נדה] among them" (1:17c). Again he uses language that can imply she has participated in some sexual immorality. Whether she will be lamented as adulterer or as victim remains a question across interpretations. The observer's judgment, however, is clear. Woman Zion's experience of suffering and her experience of God are due to her own sinfulness.

[17]Zion stretches out her hands,	that his neighbors should
but there is no one to comfort	become his foes;
her;	Jerusalem has become
the Lord has commanded against	a filthy thing among them.
Jacob	

Victimizing the Victim, Violating the Already Violated (Lam 1:18-22)

Target of ongoing charges of guilt and haunted by unrelenting anguish and isolation, Woman Zion now caves in to the surrounding confusion. As if delirious from the enormity of her suffering and grasping for some explanation as to why, Woman Zion admits that she has rebelled against God (1:18a). Like an abused, abandoned woman who has become so violated and devalued, Woman Zion now concludes it must be her own fault. Whether correct or not, that is her perception in her confused and violated state.[21] Yet, still no specificity is given to the iniquity. A tension exists between the enormity of the suffering as punishment and the lack of clarity as to exactly what she did that could merit such a punishment,[22] and though Woman Zion admits guilt, she does not sketch the nature of the sinful deed but rather turns attention to those who are affected by the punishment. Her young men and young women have gone into captivity (1:18c), and the priests and elders have perished from famine (1:19b). It is punishment enough to suffer the consequences for the judgment leveled against one's deeds; however, she also suffers because of how her own desolation has resulted in the pain and loss of others.

Acute spiritual and emotional anguish often manifest as physical symptoms. Woman Zion reports such bodily afflictions. She cries out to God that her stomach churns (1:20a). Her heart is wrung within her (1:20b). Others hear these sounds of her groaning from within (1:21a). And once again, all this is made worse by her admission that there is no one to comfort her (1:21). By her own acknowledgment, her suffering is equal to—if not worse than—death itself (1:20d). In the absence of any-

---

21. O'Connor, *Lamentations*, 27.

22. Elizabeth Boase, *The Fulfillment of Doom? The Dialogic Interaction between the Book of Lamentations and the Pre-Exilic/Early Exilic Prophetic Literature*, LHBOTS 437 (New York: T&T Clark, 2006), 214, 217.

Lamentations 1:18-22

¹⁸The Lᴏʀᴅ is in the right,
for I have rebelled against his
word;
but hear, all you peoples,
and behold my suffering;
my young women and young men
have gone into captivity.

¹⁹I called to my lovers
but they deceived me;
my priests and elders
perished in the city
while seeking food
to revive their strength.

²⁰See, O Lᴏʀᴅ, how distressed I
am;
my stomach churns,
my heart is wrung within me,
because I have been very
rebellious.

In the street the sword bereaves;
in the house it is like death.

²¹They heard how I was groaning,
with no one to comfort me.
All my enemies heard of my
trouble;
they are glad that you have
done it.
Bring on the day you have
announced,
and let them be as I am.

²²Let all their evil doing come
before you;
and deal with them
as you have dealt with me
because of all my
transgressions;
for my groans are many
and my heart is faint.

one to console her, Woman Zion's only comfort resides in her overture to God. She pleads that her enemies be dealt with the way she herself has been treated.

The lack of specificity about Zion's sin makes the lengthy and graphic depictions of her suffering as punishment difficult, if not despicable.[23] The vague nature of Woman Zion's culpability is overshadowed and far outweighed by the description of her denigration and agony. Reading this lament summons the reader to lament the theology embedded here because it further victimizes the victim and violates the already violated. If enemies are the divine instrument of punishment, her call to God to punish the enemies suggests her willingness to even reproach God. As she struggles to deal with her suffering, she also confronts and wrestles with the questions surrounding both the magnitude of her suffering and the reason for it. In the delirium of acute agony, she does give voice to the commonplace recognition of suffering as the consequence of sin. Her

23. Ibid., 173–74.

own experience, however, also nudges her to question such activity on the part of the deity, and the poignancy of Zion's suffering urges readers to question whether there is more to this text than meets the eye.

Two speakers alternate in speech across this poem in a manner that leaves Woman Zion ravaged, desolate, alone, and guilty, but Deryn Guest draws attention to the poet behind both speakers in the lament who composes this piece: "The writer himself—who has opted to describe a fallen city in terms of a fallen and justly broken woman—is the one responsible for this imagery, and yet is often the only 'character' left unexposed."[24]

Such figures as the prophets of Judah make clear who is responsible for the destruction of the nation. Their prophetic warnings are fixed upon the false prophets, the priests, the members of the royal counsel, the king, and the landholders. The patriarchal society of ancient Israel was predominantly a man's world, and though not exclusively, these men in power constituted the primary targets of the prophets' message. How is it then that Zion's destruction and guilt becomes the burden that a woman must metaphorically shoulder? Who are the ones who have not yet come to terms with their responsibility for their power-wielding games? In patriarchal society, whose acting out of hostilities often leave women and children afflicted and suffering the most? Who is the one responsible for such imagery in this text and yet remains unidentified?

Woman Zion's concluding prayer suggests the delirium and confusion that such acute suffering causes. She prays for revenge against her enemies (1:21-22). Yet, earlier she admits that her suffering by the enemies is punishment for sin. She views God as the one who has initiated this punishment but calls on God to save her from this distress. Suffering that so violates and denigrates surely impairs one's thinking and alters one's physical, emotional, and spiritual response to this kind of anguish. It challenges one's theology and alters one's self-understanding. And in the midst of such an assault, when no one is there to offer comfort, it can obscure and even obliterate one's self-worth.

24. Deryn Guest, "Hiding Behind the Naked Women in Lamentations: A Recriminative Response," *BibInt* 7 (1999): 424.

Lamentations 2

"O Daughter Zion, Who Can Heal You?" (Lam 2:13)

The Unleashing of an Angry God

The second chapter of Lamentations mirrors the first chapter in form. This second chapter contains the recitations of the observer and Woman Zion, the same two speakers encountered in the preceding lament. Similarly, the exchange that unfolds also resembles the preceding poem. Both consist of twenty-two verses and are artistically fashioned as acrostics. As in Lamentations 1, the first word of each three-line strophe begins with the letter according to the order of the Hebrew alphabet, from א, *aleph*, to ת, *taw*. Only verse 19 digresses and instead consists of a four-line strophe, likely because it concludes the long oration of one speaker.

Unlike the first lament, however, the opportunity for speech is unevenly allocated in this chapter. The observer, who speaks first, dominates the poem. His prolonged account stretches across Lamentations 2:1-19. Distinct themes divide his recitation into two sections. In the first part (Lam 2:1-10), he details God's anger as expressed in the calamity that has befallen Woman Zion. In the second part of his speech, he reflects on his own experience of Zion's destruction and Jerusalem's plight at the hands of this angry God (Lam 2:11-19). Some scholars suggest that the first-person lament in verse 11 could be heard as Woman Zion's outcry, but since this verse is part of the observer's larger recitation and because he refers to himself in a similar fashion later in this section (Lam 2:13), most scholars conclude it belongs to the second part of his speech.[1]

Woman Zion finally speaks at the very end of the poem (Lam 2:20-22). Her recitation is brief and, unlike in Lamentations 1, no exchange takes place between the observer and Woman Zion. Despite the observer's long preceding oration, Woman Zion never interrupts or addresses him. She speaks only to God with some of the same language she used at the end of Lamentations 1. This time, however, while she still voices disdain for her enemies, no hint of a confession of guilt is present as before. Woman Zion makes no admission of sin in this brief appearance.

Though uneven in length, the speeches of both the observer and Woman Zion are united in theme. God's anger, the anguish it has caused, and their respective reactions to it permeate both recitations. Moreover, the observer begins the poem by noting God's anger in the opening verse (Lam 2:1), and Woman Zion focuses on it in the concluding verse (Lam 2:22). Hence, a literary bracket spotlighting God's anger at the beginning and end of the poem encloses the thematic focus within this lament. Whereas Lamentations 1 described the calamity that took place in Zion, this poem addresses the cause for this ruin. An intemperate display of divine fury is responsible. The description of an out-of-control deity unfolds across this poem in graphic and discomfiting language that crafts a catastrophe "as vast as the sea" (Lam 2:13).

Like Lamentations 1, the date of composition of this chapter remains a point of debate. Some even read these two poems as self-contained pieces that function independently.[2] The second poem, however, clearly rests on the tragedies that have befallen Woman Zion in Lamentations 1. The charges against God in Lamentations 2 would have no context without the details of the opening lament. In addition, the same acrostic format, the dirge-like interjection "how" that opens each chapter, and the presumption that the speakers of the first poem are the speakers of this

---

1. Kathleen M. O'Connor, *Lamentations and the Tears of the World* (Maryknoll, NY: Orbis Books, 2002), 81.

2. Claus Westermann, *Lamentations: Issues and Interpretation*, trans. Charles Muenchow (Minneapolis: Fortress, 1994), 149–59; Delbert R. Hillers, *Lamentations*, AB 7A (Garden City, NY: Doubleday, 1992), 41.

second lament create a strong case for some relation between the two. Hence, the connections established by parallel forms, as well as the continuities in content and speakers, are clear. Still, the focus of each poem is distinct. The first chapter presents Woman Zion's suffering; we hear her firsthand account of this suffering and wonder whether she could possibly be responsible for all that is described. In conjunction with this tragedy, the second chapter focuses on the cause of the destruction and, without question, defines God as the cause of such immense travail. The observer is unequivocal as to God's role in bringing about Woman Zion's sorrow. Though the sentiments he expresses suggest a stance of comfort and empathy toward Woman Zion, his rhetoric discloses something else. His own experience of the surrounding misery moves him to the brink of hopelessness. In the middle of the poem, he expresses his own sense of futility within the haunting rhetorical question he directs at Woman Zion: "Who can heal you?" (Lam 2:13c).

A Battering Assault on Woman Zion (Lam 2:1-10)

Lamentations 1 ends with Woman Zion's gut-wrenching witness to her suffering that does not leave even the dispassionate, objective observer unmoved. In the first half of his recitation in the second chapter (Lam 2:1-10), he too is overcome with the scope of tragedy that Zion has experienced. With the same opening particle, "how" (איכה), he begins, but this time he is not so much expressing his incredulity as he views Woman Zion's destruction. Instead, he wrestles with disbelief how God could bring about such far-reaching violence.

"How the LORD in his anger has covered the Daughter of Zion[3] with a cloud" (Lam 2:1a).[4] Immediately, the poem suggests Zion's identity has been muddled and obscured. She is no longer recognizable by others or by God. The relationship that tied her to the Lord has been blocked

---

3. A variety of names for the land, the city, and its inhabitants occur across Lam 2: Daughter Zion (2:1a, 4b, 8a, 10a, 13c, 18b), Daughter Judah (2:2b, 5c), Zion (2:6b), Jerusalem (2:10c), Israel (2:1b, 3a, 5), Jacob (2:2a, 3c), and Daughter Jerusalem (2:13b, 15b).

4. I digress here from the NRSV translation, "How the Lord in his anger has humiliated daughter Zion!" (2:1a), because the verb עוב is a hapax legomenon, likely a *hiphil* verb related to the noun עב "cloud," hence "covered with a cloud"; Johan Renkema, *Lamentations*, trans. Brian Doyle, HCOT (Leuven: Peeters, 1998), 216; Robert B. Salters, *Lamentations: A Critical and Exegetical Commentary*, ICC (New York: T&T Clark, 1994), 112; F. W. Dobbs-Allsopp, *Lamentations*, IBC (Louisville: Westminster John Knox, 2002), 80; Westermann, *Lamentations*, 140.

Lamentations 2:1-10

2:1How the Lord in his anger
     has humiliated daughter Zion!
He has thrown down from heaven
          to earth
      the splendor of Israel;
he has not remembered his footstool
     in the day of his anger.

2The Lord has destroyed without
          mercy
  all the dwellings of Jacob;
in his wrath he has broken down
     the strongholds of daughter
          Judah;
he has brought down to the
          ground in dishonor
      the kingdom and its rulers.

3He has cut down in fierce anger
  all the might of Israel;
he has withdrawn his right hand
          from them
     in the face of the enemy;

he has burned like a flaming fire
     in Jacob,
     consuming all around.

4He has bent his bow like an
          enemy,
  with his right hand set like a
          foe;
he has killed all in whom we took
          pride
     in the tent of daughter Zion;
he has poured out his fury like
          fire.

5The Lord has become like an
          enemy;
  he has destroyed Israel.
He has destoyed all its palaces,
     laid in ruins its strongholds,
and multiplied in daughter Judah
     mourning and lamentation.

6He has broken down his booth
     like a garden,

out. This clouding suggests "a murky barrier"[5] has been cast over Zion so as to conceal and separate her from the One who first called her by name. Following this introduction to the divine discipline that appears to cut Zion off from what once surrounded her, a disturbing litany of verbs (Lam 2:1-8) describes God's battering assault upon her and her inhabitants. A literal translation of the Hebrew suggests the viciousness and relentlessness of the divine tirade: "he threw down" (2:1b), "he swallowed up" (2:2a, 5ab, 8b),[6] "he has broken down" (2:2b), "he has cut down" (2:3a), "he burned" (2:3c), "he has killed" (2:4c), "he destroyed" (2:5a), "he poured out " (2:4d), "he spurned" (2:6d), "he scorned" (2:7a), and "he delivered into the hands of the enemy" (2:7b). As if obsessed

---

5. O'Connor, *Lamentations*, 33.
6. The verb here is בלע, translated as "to destroy" in NRSV (2:2a), but it also means "to consume" or "to swallow up" and occurs in 2:2a, 5ab, 8b, 16b.

he has destroyed his tabernacle;
the Lord has abolished in Zion
    festival and sabbath,
and in his fierce indignation has
    spurned
    king and priest.

⁷The Lord has scorned his altar,
    disowned his sanctuary;
he has delivered into the hand of
    the enemy
    the walls of her palaces;
a clamor was raised in the house
    of the Lord
    as on a day of festival.

⁸The Lord determined to lay in
    ruins
    the wall of daughter Zion;
he stretched the line;
    he did not withhold his hand
        from destroying;

he caused rampart and wall to
    lament;
    they languish together.

⁹Her gates have sunk into the
    ground;
    he has ruined and broken her
        bars;
her king and princes are among
    the nations;
    guidance is no more,
and her prophets obtain
    no vision from the Lord.

¹⁰The elders of daughter Zion
    sit on the ground in silence;
they have thrown dust on their
    heads
    and put on sackcloth;
the young girls of Jerusalem
    have bowed their heads to the
        ground.

with destruction, or with an insatiable hunger for revenge, or just plain out of control, the Lord's ceaseless assault multiplies the pain and misery to incalculable extremes. This unbearable harm and misery echo in the observer's report of Woman Zion's iterative response of "mourning and lamentation" (Lam 2:5c).

In the past, the right hand of God was an image that saved by sheltering the people and restraining the enemy (Exod 15:6, 12; Deut 26:8; Ps 89:13; Isa 41:10), but now, the Holy One has "withdrawn his right hand from them in the face of the enemy" (Lam 2:3b). Unprotected, Zion now becomes easy prey for those ready to plunder. Moreover, God has become "like an enemy" (Lam 2:4a, 5a). Scholars debate whether the Hebrew particle כ before the word "enemy" describing God is to be read as a comparison, "like an enemy," or as an asseverative particle asserting that God is "the enemy." Miriam Bier, however, wisely notes that "it matters not one whit whether YHWH is in fact an enemy, or is merely behaving like an enemy. The outcome they experience—starvation, fire, destruction, death—is the same."[7]

The accusation that God is "like an enemy" responsible for destruction is expanded in the next verse (Lam 2:4), which lays bare the ultimate horror of God's unbridled rage. "God has slain all who were pleasing to the eye" (Lam 2:4).[8] The destruction of the city calls for lamentation, but God's deliberate slaying of Jerusalem's inhabitants bespeaks a horror impossible to explain and problematic for theodicy. The image of God "swallowing up" is repeated five times in this lament (Lam 2:2a, 5ab, 8b, 16b). "The Lord has destroyed ['swallowed up'[9]] without mercy all the dwellings of Jacob" (Lam 2:2a); this narrates God's consumption of the physical structures that define Zion. Furthermore, God has "swallowed up Israel" (Lam 2:5a).[10] This carnage, however, is not just the result of unrestrained impulse from an angry deity.

The Divine Plan for Destruction

"The Lord determined to lay in ruins the wall of daughter Zion" (Lam 2:8). The Hebrew word חשב ("to determine") indicates forethought and intention. Nothing is spontaneous here. The observer narrates that God carefully planned and carried out this bloody devastation with precision and premeditation. All that Zion stood for has been leveled. Such a complete and comprehensive destruction suggests a blueprint executed with an extravagance of violence. In addition, any means of contact with the deity that might reunite the people with God has been demolished. The elements of worship—the tabernacle, the altar, the sanctuary, and even the cultic opportunity for festival and the Sabbath—have all been earmarked for destruction (Lam 2:6-7a). The institutions associated with the governance and protection of the population—palaces and strongholds—have been "laid in ruins" (Lam 2:5b). All protective structures, such as the wall surrounding the city along with the rampart and the gates, have disappeared into the ground (Lam 2:8-9a). Those once re-

7. Miriam J. Bier, *'Perhaps There Is Hope': Reading Lamentations as a Polyphony of Pain, Penitence, and Protest*, LHBOTS (New York: Bloomsbury T&T Clark, 2015), 81.

8. Though the NRSV translates ויהרג כל מחמדי־עין, "he has killed all in whom we took pride," a more literal translation of the Hebrew renders "He [God] has slain all who were pleasing to the eye" (2:4c).

9. Refer to footnote 6, p. 22.

10. Again, digressing from the NRSV here, the translation preferred is "to swallow up" in order to capture the nuances of Woman Zion's accusations against the deity in vv. 20-22.

sponsible for governing authority in Zion—kings and princes—have vanished or "are among the nations" (Lam 2:9c).

The Cry of the Poor (Lam 2:11-19)

With verse 11, a major shift in the focus and demeanor of the observer occurs. While his voice continues to dominate the poem, he no longer speaks about God's destruction and its unimaginable consequences for Jerusalem and the inhabitants. Three distinct concerns define the rest of his speech. First, his objective reporting gives way to a deeply personal account. For the first time, with first-person speech, he testifies to the physical and emotional effect of this disaster upon himself (Lam 2:11-12). Then, turning his attention to Woman Zion (Lam 2:13-17), he ponders aloud with her who or what might be to blame for the horror that has ensued. He is heard trying to answer the question with which he began the lament in both Lamentations 1 and Lamentations 2: "How?" How could this happen and how could God do this? He also indirectly wrestles the question that all who suffer confront: "Why?" Finally, as if to believe that this destruction is reversible, he offers advice to Woman Zion (Lam 2:18-19). As if her suffering could be curtailed, the observer urges Woman Zion to take action.

When the observer ceases only to objectively report and opens himself up to experience the depth of Woman Zion's pain, her trauma begins to invade his feeling life. Emotional and physical symptoms indicate this shift. The horrors of her experience permeate his defenses and horrify him. As he begins to identify with the afflicted inhabitants, his eyes like hers (1:2a) "are spent with weeping" (Lam 2:11). He allows himself to finally feel the agony of what he has witnessed. That his gut-wrenching emotion gives way to his physical symptoms testifies to the ancients' belief that "the inner organs are generally the center of human emotion."[11] His stomach churns and bile pours out on the ground as he beholds the scope and gravity of the city's devastation and the massacre of its inhabitants (Lam 2:11).

What prompts this abrupt transition in the observer's stance? Why does he now empathize and raise his own outcry in response to the tragedy about which he so dispassionately reported in Lamentations 1? While he finds the destruction of the people reprehensible, the suffering and death of innocent infants and children apparently ruptures all his defenses (Lam 2:11c). For the first time, he seems unable to cope in the face of the starvation and suffering of the most innocent and helpless

---

11. Dianne Bergant, *Lamentations*, AOTC (Nashville: Abingdon, 2003), 69.

¹¹My eyes are spent with
　　weeping;
　my stomach churns;
　my bile is poured out on the
　　ground
　　because of the destruction of
　　　my people,
　because infants and babes faint
　　in the streets of the city.

¹²They cry to their mothers,
　　"Where is bread and wine?"
　as they faint like the wounded
　　in the streets of the city,
　as their life is poured out
　　on their mother's bosom.

¹³What can I say for you, to what
　　compare you,
　　O daughter Jerusalem?

To what can I liken you, that I may
　　comfort you,
　　O virgin daughter Zion?
For vast as the sea is your ruin;
　　who can heal you?

¹⁴Your prophets have seen for you
　　false and deceptive visions;
　they have not exposed your iniquity
　　to restore your fortunes,
　but have seen oracles for you
　　that are false and misleading.

¹⁵All who pass along the way
　　clap their hands at you;
　they hiss and wag their heads
　　at daughter Jerusalem;
　"Is this the city that was called
　　the perfection of beauty,
　　the joy of all the earth?"

victims. He hears their "cry to their mothers" (Lam 2:12) asking for bread and for something to drink, yet he knows there is nothing to offer. The sight of them lying faint in the streets makes their vulnerability stark and unbearable (Lam 2:11c). Though their lives have hardly begun, these infants know only the pain of starvation (Lam 2:12a). Though they were once viewed as the hope for the nation, they now lack any prospect of a future. They can only cry out to their mothers who have nothing to offer (Lam 2:12a). They die at their mothers' breasts, the very place where they should receive nourishment for life (Lam 2:12c). Though no mention is made of their suffering, mothers who behold their starving, emaciated infants must be out of their minds with grief and helplessness.

A Loss of Words, Beyond Repair

This display of suffering children is too much for the observer. He now turns to Woman Zion and confesses that he is at a loss for words: "What can I say for you, to what compare you, O daughter Jerusalem? To what can I liken you, that I may comfort you, O virgin daughter Zion?" (Lam 2:13ab). For the first time, he addresses her with a tenderness that mirrors his empathic response to her suffering. Yet the answer to his rhe-

¹⁶All your enemies
> open their mouths against you;
they hiss, they gnash their teeth,
they cry: "We have devoured
> > her!
Ah, this is the day we longed for;
> at last we have seen it!"

¹⁷The LORD has done what he
> purposed,
> he has carried out his threat;
as he ordained long ago,
> he has demolished without
> > pity;
he has made the enemy rejoice
> over you,
> and exalted the might of your
> > foes.

¹⁸Cry aloud to the Lord!
> O wall of daughter Zion!
Let tears stream down like a
> torrent
> day and night!
Give yourself no rest,
> your eyes no respite!

¹⁹Arise, cry out in the night,
> at the beginning of the
> > watches!
Pour out your heart like water
> before the presence of the
> > Lord!
Lift your hands to him
> for the lives of your children,
who faint for hunger
> at the head of every street.

torical questions is clear. There is no answer. No words exist to accurately describe what he has witnessed and felt. Though in Lamentations 1 he enlisted the metaphor of an abused woman and perhaps even labeled her an adulteress to narrate Zion's decimation, he now confesses that words fail him. As he allows himself to enter the realm of her experience, what he witnesses is simply beyond narration. Still, he struggles to find words to express what he has encountered. While no image is suitable for Woman Zion herself, he compares her ruin to the vastness of the sea (Lam 2:13c). It is a fitting image. From the shore, the sea may appear boundless, as its farthest limits often merge on the horizon with the sky. That Zion's ruin is comparable to such an infinite expanse prompts him to ask a final rhetorical question: "who can heal you?" (Lam 2:13c). Salters suggests that his final inquiry implies that "she is beyond repair" in the observer's eyes,[12] and if the possibility that someone could heal her exists, then it is the One who has already been indicted as having willfully conducted the assault. Though highly problematic, the possibility of turning to the Lord as the one who can heal her will be the basis of the advice he gives to Woman Zion at the conclusion of his speech.

12. Salters, *Lamentations*, 154.

Prayer from the Ruins

When I pray with Lamentations I try to find some place inside myself where I can identify with this suffering, the depth of this grief and loss. And I cannot. My life is so privileged, my anxieties of my own making. I have a home, food, water, clothing, beauty around me in many forms, the love of friends and family, security, comfort, safety. I have little cause for lament. And yet.

The world around me, near and far, is filled with suffering—hunger, thirst, disease, homelessness, violence, racism, oppression. This is my world and I am part of it and so I do have cause to lament, to raise my prayer. Don't we all feel powerless in the face of all the suffering that we see, even if it is only in the news? And don't we turn our faces from it when it comes close? In our cities it is the homeless, the men and women, even families, begging on the corner for spare change who confront us with suffering like that we find in Lamentations. People who have lost everything but their lives. "Away! Unclean!" a voice inside us says: "Away! Away! Do not touch" (Lam 4:15).

And now in our time there is a growing host of newly dispossessed people, people who can rightly own the whole of Lamentations, who have "gone into exile with suffering and hard servitude," living now "among the nations and finding no resting place"—the myriad refugees from nations at war in the Middle East and Africa, people fleeing bombs, militias, starvation, forced conscription, their communities in ruins. They stretch out their hands and there is no one to comfort them (1:17); they are turned away and walls are built to keep them out. We see them nightly on the news, their panic, their desperate seeking for a place to land, to live. "They became fugitives and wanderers; it was said among the nations 'They shall stay here no longer'" (Lam 4:15).

Again, I think we feel helpless in the face of so massive and desperate a tide of suffering. What can we do? Of course there are many answers to that question—legislation, community organizing, charity, political involvement, and all of these must be employed. But there is also a place for prayer here, communal prayers of petition like those we raise in worship services, yes, but also something more. I think about this book, Lamentations, and its liturgical function. The image of this defeated people in Jerusalem, seeking to rebuild a life in the ruins of their own former greatness, with so many of their numbers missing, in exile. How they gathered to remember, to reflect, to examine their history, to mourn, to cry out, to plead, to pray, to hope, to envision a future restored. Maybe this is a practice that we need to engage in today, including those of us who have not been directly affected by war and famine and military occupation. If we join our prayer to the prayer of those who have lost their homes, their families, their livelihood, even their country and the comfort of their culture, perhaps something new can rise from this prayer. By turning away from their suffering I think I am protecting myself from somehow becoming drawn into their pain. But what if by opening ourselves to this suffering we will be drawn into kinship with those who suffer and ourselves be changed? What if opening in prayer *with them* to their plight we are able to open other spaces, spaces that inch by inch can grow and lead to larger openings, a welcome, a place to rest, to find comfort, to envision a future.

If my lament is not a prayer, it is simply a complaint, a cry of grief or pain or rage that rises like smoke from a fire and eventually dissipates in the air. But if it becomes a prayer and is joined to many voices in prayer, then it has power, staying power, active power, the power to change. The book of Lamentations is a prayer, and not just any prayer, but a communal prayer, the prayer of a people, a prayer of memory and hope. Imagine the power that could ensue from reclaiming this kind of prayer in our own time, from joining diverse communities to face this suffering together and ultimately to confront its causes.

Jill Marshall

Assigning Blame: Prophets, Enemies, God, and the Woman

The observer turns his attention to assigning blame for this experience of destruction that now has touched him so deeply. Three candidates emerge in his speech. First, he charges Zion's prophets with failing to do their job and thus contributing to her downfall. He argues that they offered only "false and deceptive visions" (Lam 2:14a), obscuring the iniquity from which Woman Zion could have then retreated. Some scholars note that here the observer implies Woman Zion sinned, but only to magnify the failings of her prophets.[13] He also suggests she would have been able to be restored had the prophets been responsible (Lam 2:14b). Because these religious officials failed in their duty, Zion and its inhabitants have been misled. All suffer for the irresponsibility and false pronouncements of these prophets. That the prophets' failure led to

---

13. See Iain Provan, *Lamentations*, New Century Bible Commentary (Grand Rapids: Eerdmans, 1991), 73, and Robin A. Parry, *Lamentations*, THOTC (Grand Rapids: Eerdmans, 2010), 80.

Zion's destruction raises questions. Why would a nation receive punishment "whose prophets failed to do their job and warn her to change her ways before it was too late?"[14] Even after her destruction, Woman Zion continues to incur the mockery and shaming of "all who pass along the way . . . ; they hiss and wag their heads at daughter Jerusalem" (Lam 2:15ab) because the prophets led her astray. Those passing by hurl insults at her, recalling the glory that once surrounded her: "Is this the city that was called the perfection of beauty, the joy of all the earth?" (Lam 2:15c). Such mockery only deepens the pain and shame of her current state.

Next, the observer targets Zion's enemies as blameworthy for the current ruins. He describes their claim of success at overpowering her. They declare they have wreaked their havoc in a way that disgraces her. The images are utterly physical, abusive, and humiliating. They "open their mouths" (Lam 2:16a) against her, they "gnash their teeth" (Lam 2:16b), and they cry that they "have devoured her" (Lam 2:16b). Moreover, the enemies inject these very physical assertions of her subjugation with a discomfiting emotional remark. They declare that they have "longed for" this day (Lam 2:16c). Such longing on the part of her enemies suggests their cruel anticipation of her humiliation and destruction.

Finally, a third party is accused for the current catastrophe surrounding both the observer and Woman Zion. The observer reverts back to blaming God, this time in a somewhat more righteous manner than described in the earlier part of his speech. He claims that the Lord has done exactly as had been proposed. Here he insinuates that Zion and all who inhabited her knew from the beginning this would be the result of unrepented sin. While he avoids the difficult images with which he described God's contested deeds in the earlier part of the poem, he suggests here a lack of control on the Lord's part: "he has demolished without pity" (Lam 2:17b). Divine punishment in the face of unrepented iniquity was clear within the covenantal agreement, but the unrestrained assault that turns even innocent babies into victims raises questions about both the covenant and its parties. In addition, the observer claims again that though the enemies appeared responsible for Zion's fate, they were mere instruments. God enlisted these vicious agents to bring mother Zion to her knees. The enemies were not only victorious but also celebratory. God enabled the enemy to "rejoice" (Lam 2:17c) in the face of her downfall, and the Lord even "exalted the might of [her] foes" (Lam 2:17d) about what her enemy had plundered. As if her destruction were not enough,

---

14. Bier, *'Perhaps There Is Hope,'* 93.

the divinely sanctioned celebration of these victorious foes further dis-honored the burned and battered Zion.

A desperation echoes across the observer's attempts to explain the unexplainable. He shifts his finger, pointing from God in the first part of his speech (Lam 2:1-10), to the false prophets (Lam 2:14), to Zion's ene-mies (Lam 2:16), and ultimately back to God (Lam 2:17). With Zion, he struggles with the unanswerable questions—"How?" and "Why?"—in the face of incalculable suffering. Yet, he ends his litany of blame in the same place he began. In the context of covenant, because he reasserts that God is at the helm of this annihilating fury, he also implies that Zion has sinned. Like Job's friends whose attempts to comfort actually turn blame on the righteous man, the observer's attempts at empathic comfort ultimately assign responsibility for Woman Zion's destruction to her very self.

A Perilous Proposal That Further Endangers the Victim

On the one hand, he is convinced that she in incomparable, that her ruin is boundless, and that her healing is beyond repair. On the other hand, though the observer has supposedly felt her pain, he still resorts to the unthinkable. In the conclusion of his long speech, he calls on suf-fering Zion to take action (Lam 2:18-19). Though he appeared to comfort her, and may even be in a position to act on her behalf, instead he insists she herself do something. Despite her encumbered, suffering state, she is to engage in a last-ditch effort to end the calamity. The observer does not just suggest she do something to remedy the situation; he com-mands her to do it. With a barrage of imperatives, he directs Woman Zion to do the only thing he considers capable of stemming the mount-ing aftermath of her destruction. He directs the woman city to turn her attention to God and "cry aloud" (Lam 2:18a), "shed tears" (Lam 2:18b),[15] "give yourself no rest" (Lam 2:18c), "arise" (Lam 2:19a), "cry out in the night" (Lam 2:19a), "pour out your heart" (Lam 2:19b), and "lift up your hands" (Lam 2:19c). Thus he orders her to make an emotional display before the Lord, to be ceaseless in this spectacle, to resist even resting, and be demonstrative as in a prayerful appeal. Despite her brokenness, Woman Zion is urged to employ her whole being—with hands raised, tears streaming, voice crying out, and heart uplifted. She is to act with

---

15. Ulrich Berges, "The Violence of God in the Book of Lamentations," in *One Text, a Thousand Methods: Studies in Memory of Sjef van Tilborg,* ed. Patrick Chatelion Counet and Ulrich Berges (Boston: Brill, 2005), 35.

all her might in order to persuade the all-powerful God to stop acting against her. The observer's directives to her bear no hint of her need to repent before the Lord.[16] Nothing he advises suggests she must mend a broken relationship. Rather, the observer clearly compels her to assume the humble posture of one making supplication.

Concluding his instructions to her, the observer lays bare what motivates him and what he intends will galvanize her. He already made clear that the tragedy of innocent children becoming victims was beyond his physical and emotional tolerance (Lam 2:11c-12). Still, he recites again the scandal of dying children on display so publically "at the head of every street" (Lam 2:19). Despite his repulsion at the sight, he intends to play on Woman Zion's maternal instincts in order to prompt her action. Indeed, the affliction of infants and children by God is utterly unacceptable. The absence of his abhorrence and disdain when Woman Zion is abused, raped, and dismantled beyond recognition, however, is also utterly unacceptable. The tortured, overpowered, and deeply wounded Woman Zion is urged—even expected—to stem the violence herself. She, the victim, is urged to turn to the One identified as abuser and seek resolution. The metaphoric Woman Zion who has been debased, violated, and "swallowed up" by her attacker is encouraged to return to her torturer for relief. Present here is a theological tension that so many identify and wrestle with. Can this encounter be read theodotically or only anti-theodotically?[17] The real unease that permeates this poem, however, is also a dis-ease. It resides in the duplication of a well-known pattern surrounding the violence in relationships. Linafeldt astutely offers a summary diagnosis: "The notion of an abused and violated woman turning for help to her abuser, and the one who abused her children, should inspire in the modern reader something less than the notion of [God's] gracious intervention."[18]

---

16. Dobbs-Alsopp, *Lamentations*, 79; Tod Linafelt, *Surviving Lamentations: Catastrophe, Lament, and Protest in the Afterlife of a Biblical Book* (Chicago: University of Chicago Press, 2000), 100; and Elizabeth Boase, *The Fulfillment of Doom? The Dialogic Interaction between the Book of Lamentations and the Pre-Exilic/Early Exilic Prophetic Literature*, LHBOTS 437 (New York: T&T Clark, 2006), 190.

17. Bier, in *'Perhaps There Is Hope,'* addresses the long-debated question of whether Lamentations hosts a consistent theology throughout. She persuasively argues that Lamentations, read as a polyphony of voices, accommodates both theodotic and anti-theodotic sentiments often in tension and gives rise to theodotic and anti-theodotic interpretations according to the perspectives of readers.

18. Linafelt, *Surviving Lamentations*, 55.

The Strength of a Community

What allows an abused woman to slice through the silence that so frequently surrounds abuse and speak up? Is it courage, despair, or simply having nothing left to lose that allows Zion to confront God (Lam 2:20)? All too many women continue to suffer abuse in the workplace. Unfortunately, this was my situation as I endured abusive behavior from a boss for a year and a half before I was able to report him. My workplace was not a supportive environment. Therefore, I knew I would be even more vulnerable if I made a report without proof; otherwise my accusation would merely result in a "he said/ she said" volley. I managed to remain in the situation because of an incredible network of support outside my work. However, there was never any question for me that I would speak up; instead, it was about how and when to do so.

As a religious sister, I was aware that I had an entire group of experienced and wise women behind me that gave me more security than others might feel. It gave me the courage to stay in the situation long enough to report the abuse for the protection and safety of others. A single mom who needed a job was far more vulnerable to abusive behavior than I was. As a sister, I knew I could leave anytime if it became too much, which also helped free me to stay. The real source of my strength, however, was my sisters—both within my own community and in other communities. Numerous sisters listened to each inappropriate encounter with my boss, allowed me to process the confusion and fear I felt, offered helpful advice, and strategized with me how I should respond until I could ultimately report him. One sister in particular was my spiritual director and guide; she assisted me by constantly asking me questions: How would I know if it was time to remove myself from the situation? How would I know if I was being hurt too badly by the experience? This was valuable because it kept the reality that I *was* harmed by the experience before me. It kept me from negating the pain of the experience and helped me look at it with honesty and regularity. Together these sisters loved me, affirmed me, expressed concern on my behalf, and kept possibilities alive in me. Their questions and insights gave me the gift of options—and therefore choice—which also freed me to be deliberate and creative in working against a coercive working environment. I was able to find ways to push back well before I had the proof I needed to report the abuse. My answer to my spiritual director's questions was that I would know it was time for me to me to leave when I could no longer see creative possibilities for myself and others in that excruciating work environment. It allowed me to stay until I finally had a witness.

  While I did address God with an occasional, "Work with me here," unlike Zion, I did not blame God for the abuse I experienced. But to be fair, unlike Zion, I was not subject to a theology that defined the experience of evil or wrongdoing as punishment for something I did. Instead, I am convinced that God guided me through this time with my network of sisterly support. I experienced rich prayer and God felt close throughout those years. I wonder if God would have seemed absent if I had been alone in such a situation.

Sarah Kohles

The Victim Rises Up to Confront Her Abuser (Lam 2:20-22)

Urged by the observer to turn to God, Woman Zion now speaks. Though instructed to be emotional, to pour out her tears, to plead and cry and assume the posture of a desperate woman supplicant, she does otherwise. As she begins, she calls on God to pay attention and ponder what he has done. In essence, she boldly invites God to do some self-reflection: "Look, O Lord, and consider! To whom have you done this?" (Lam 2:20). In contrast to God's loss of control and excess of violent displays, Woman Zion practices a disciplined composure with measured and direct speech and employs an economy of words. No emotional outpouring accompanies her recitation. As a strong woman who has given up being a victim, and who has abandoned self-blame before her abuser, she confronts the Lord. With words aimed directly at her torturer, she paints a canvas portraying God's campaign of carnage with graphic images that eclipse the horror already narrated by the observer. Not only have infants died at mothers' breasts, but "women eat their offspring, the children they have borne" (Lam 2:20). The loss of maternal instinct that would allow a mother to eat her children has elsewhere been portrayed (2 Kgs 6:20-31), but cannibalizing one's children is not the consequence of a mere gustatory response resulting from famine.[19] Rather, the image of mothers consuming their children serves as exponent of how extreme and oppressive social conditions had become as a result of this deity's

19. See Gina Hens-Piazza, *Nameless, Blameless and without Shame: Two Cannibal Mothers before a King*, Interfaces (Collegeville, MN: Liturgical Press, 2003), 85–87, for a cultural exposition on cannibalism and how its manifestation coincides with the prevailing socio-political system.

Lamentations 2:20-22

²⁰Look, O LORD, and consider!
  To whom have you done this?
Should women eat their offspring,
  the children they have borne?
Should priest and prophet be killed
  in the sanctuary of the Lord?

²¹The young and the old are lying
  on the ground in the streets;
my young women and my young
    men
  have fallen by the sword;

in the day of your anger you have
    killed them,
  slaughtering without mercy.

²²You invited my enemies from all
    around
  as if for a day of festival;
and on the day of the anger of the
    LORD
  no one escaped or survived;
those whom I bore and reared
  my enemy has destroyed.

destruction. With the Lord who has wielded such monstrous power amid the powerless lies responsibility for such horrors. Moreover, God's own behavior has been persistently described and thus experienced as "swallowing up" the people and their well-being (Lam 2:2a, 5ab, 8b, 16b). Hence, mothers eating their own babies results from the circumstances narrated as God "swallowing up" his own people. In addition, Woman Zion uses the image of God "slaughtering" her inhabitants. The word "slaughtering" carries the connotation of killing for food. In Hebrew, the word "slaughter" (טבחת) is typically enlisted to describe the killing of animals for meat (Gen 43:16; Exod 21:37; 1 Sam 25:11). Hence, when used metaphorically for the destruction of humanity, it not only bespeaks of an act of cruelty but even suggests intention of consumption.[20] As one scholar observes, "A fundamental difference between Zion and Yahweh has to be noted: they [the people] were forced to do what they did because he did not restrain his wrath but completed his anger."[21] Women are consuming their children because the Lord has consumed the people.

Responsibility for the Consequences of Brutality

Next, she addresses the scope of this rampage. Despite her broken, violated core, Woman Zion's direct and straightforward recitation suggests she has found the courage to confront her aggressor with the brutal consequences of his deeds. Not only have children died terrible deaths,

20. Berges, "The Violence of God," 39.
21. Ibid., 38.

but the city is also strewn with the bodies of young and old, laying lifeless in the streets. The hope of the future—young women and young men along with priest and prophet—have all been killed. Fearless and without qualification, she cites God's violence three times. "You have killed," "slaughtering," and "without mercy" (Lam 2:21c). Like an actual human victim, the truth she speaks seems to fuel her confidence as she confronts her attacker. Finally, she holds God responsible for what her enemies have been able to accomplish in shaming and overcoming her. She notes that God summoned her enemies to contribute to her demise as if they were celebrating a festival. Invited by God, these hostile forces treated the execution of her citizens as a celebration (Lam 2:22). As a result, "no one escaped or survived" (Lam 2:22c), but her final pronouncement does not indict these other nations; instead, the pronouncement may well be heard as ultimately directed at God. Her concluding reference to "enemy" (Lam 2:22c) is congruent with the observer's earlier use of the term, where twice he portrayed God as "like an enemy" (Lam 2:4, 5). Though Woman Zion's use of the term here comes on the heels of pointing to her enemies as the Lord's instruments of destruction (Lam 2:22a), her closing words enlist "enemy" in the singular form. She narrates with striking clarity both the scope of destruction and the one she deems responsible for it. Consistent with all that she has said in this brief response, ultimately God is cast as her foe:[22] "All whom I bore and reared, my enemy has destroyed" (Lam 2:23c).[23]

This chapter ends unlike all the other chapters in Lamentations. No suggestion of repentance that could foster hope comes to the fore. No positive shift in the future is anticipated as relief. No optimism resides in the theology here. Some scholars have noted that at least the observer tried to serve as source of comfort, in contrast to the iterative observations in Lamentations 1 where "there is no one to comfort her" (1:2, 7, 9, 16, 17, 21). The observer, however, dominates the speech here. Though he gives voice to her suffering and pain, he actually subsumes the female

---

22. Archie Chi Chung Lee, "Mothers Bewailing: Reading Lamentations," in *Her Master's Tools? Feminist and Postcolonial Engagements of Historical-Critical Discourse*, ed. Caroline Vander Stichele and Todd C. Penner, GPBS 9 (Atlanta: SBL Press, 2005), 207; Berges, "The Violence of God," 39.

23. I am reading "enemy" as singular with MT against the plural in the Peshitta and Targum. Whether "enemy" refers to those hostile nations who are the instrument of divine wrath or to the Lord is immaterial. Woman Zion aims her charge of injustice at God.

account of her own experience. Hence, the subjective female narrative of what has occurred for her is reduced to a brief response and confined to the conclusion. This marginalization of her words reinforces the presiding notion that woman cannot speak for herself. Moreover, before she actually has a chance to say something, the observer has instructed her in exactly what she should say and how she should say it. His instruction that she should turn to God unfortunately coincides with a more contemporary image of a stereotypical weeping hysterical female who takes full responsibility for all the pain she has endured. The observer, who holds God responsible for the destruction, never dares to suggest that the Lord has acted well beyond God's own parameters of justice and equity. Instead, Woman Zion is the one who boldly confronts the Lord—with a precision and brevity of speech that indict God.

This instance is the last time Woman Zion's voice is heard, though she is referenced briefly again in Lamentations 4 (4:3, 6, 10, 22b). She now seems to be written out of the text. Some readers might be tempted to read that as consequence for her affront to the Lord: she is never heard from again. One could also conclude that, like the children who asked for bread and received no answer (Lam 2:12a), Woman Zion is similarly ignored after her brief oration. Hence, God's lack of response to her courageous speech in Lamentations 2:20-22 further denigrates her. Another reading, however, is also possible. Perhaps the concluding bold overture by this city woman, who, despite her brokenness, has mustered the strength to move past her victimhood and face the one defined as her abuser, is enough to silence God.

Lamentations 3

"Does the Lord Not See?"
(Lam 3:36)

A "Strong Man" Displays a Lack of Strength

Situated in the center of the five poems that comprise Lamentations, this third chapter is often earmarked as the saving high point of the book. In its central position, it expresses the only message of hope heard within the five chapters. Some scholars view the narratives of tumult and suffering in the surrounding chapters as being quelled and steadied by the assurances of this third lament.[1] Whether or not this reputation is accurate remains to be seen.

Unlike Lamentations 1 and 2 that unfold through the exchanges of two speakers, the observer and Woman Zion, this chapter features only one male voice. In this first-person account, what he relates fixes attention

---

1. Norman K. Gottwald, *Studies in the Book of Lamentations* (Chicago: A. R. Allenson, 1954), 94–95; Delbert R. Hillers, *Lamentations*, AB 7A (New York: Doubleday, 1992), 64; Brevard S. Childs, *Introduction to the Old Testament as Scripture* (Philadelphia: Fortress, 1979), 594; Jeffrey Howard Tigay, Alan Cooper, and Bathja Bayer, "Lamentations, Book of," in *Encyclopedia Judaica*, ed. Fred Skolnik and Michael Berenbaum, 2nd ed., vol. 12 (Detroit: Macmillan, 2007), 446; Duane A. Garrett and Paul R. House, *Song of Songs/Lamentations*, WBC 23B (Nashville: Nelson, 2004), 429.

solely upon himself and his experience of the destruction. In a few instances, he speaks to and on behalf of the community that also has encountered this tragedy. In the opening verse, he identifies himself as the
גבר, one of several Hebrew words for "man" and most often related to
the notion of strength.[2] Hence, he will be referred to as the "strong man"
here.[3] Because some of the poem's imagery echoes the onslaughts of warfare, the reference to himself as a "strong man" (גבר) conjures the image
of a mighty soldier and builds expectations of protection. On the heels of
Woman Zion's summation of the horrors that she and her children have
undergone, one might envision this strong man to play a key role in the
rescue and reversal from such desperate straits. His expressions of hope
throughout the poem would encourage such expectations, if they were
not undercut by his frequent lapses into hopelessness. Unfortunately,
this vacillation between declarations of confidence and a sense of being
utterly distraught permeates the verses and thus defines the tone of this
third lament. The strong man who claims to be weakened—and even
teeters on the brink of death—crafts a paradoxical air rather than an
atmosphere of safety and assurance.

A Triple Acrostic: Structure and Form

Though the chapter unfolds as an acrostic, it claims distinctiveness in
form from the earlier poems. Fashioned as a triple acrostic, a successive
letter of the alphabet introduces the beginning word of each of three
successive lines.[4] One might characterize the poem as an acrostic in the
extreme. Such an attempt at order and control from the mouth of the
mighty soldier may well be heard as a desperate gesture to constrain
the uncontrollable assaults and chaos that accompany his experience of
destruction, but this intensely ordered form is at odds with the content of
his speech, for his descriptions will reveal that his exterior circumstances
lay in utter disarray and that his own interior response is riddled with
ambiguity.

While two laments dominate the structure of the poem (Lam 3:1-20,
43-66), other units intervene and complicate the framework. Verses 21-24

---

2. I am following Francis Brown, et al., *A Hebrew and English Lexicon of the Old Testament: With an Appendix, Containing the Biblical Aramaic* (Oxford: Clarendon, 1979), 150.

3. See Kathleen M. O'Connor, *Lamentations and the Tears of the World* (Maryknoll,
NY: Orbis Books, 2002), 44.

4. Adele Berlin, *Lamentations* (Louisville: Westminster John Knox, 2002), 85.

follow the first lament, narrating reasons for hope while marking a dramatic shift in tone. An introspective reflection follows in 3:25-39, as the speaker struggles to reconcile his experience with his theology. A summons to the community (3:40-42) bolsters the halting theological conclusions at which he has arrived. But abruptly, the optimism dissipates on further reflection. Again, the fleeting hope succumbs to the weight of a second lament (3:43-66). Both content and theme help to define these units. The threefold pattern of the acrostic is, however, interrupted by these divisions, mirroring the strong man's inner turmoil that interrupts his faltering overtures to fashion hope.[5]

The Strong Man Confesses His Own Vulnerability (Lam 3:1-20)

Unlike the first two poems that open with the interrogative "how" (איכה), exclaiming disbelief at what they experienced, this lament begins with a first-person declaration about the speaker himself: הגבר אבי, "I am the man of strength" (3:1).[6] Still, this seemingly confident self-declaration might also seek to address the scope and magnitude of what has occurred. Not even he, the strong man, is able to suppress the attack by "the rod of God's wrath" (3:1). Clarification of whose wrath is being referred to remains unspecified initially. Instead, in the verses that follow, metaphors portray this attacker as the antithesis of a shepherd, a mighty militarist, and a relentless assailant. Some scholars have noted that the would-be shepherd who functions in Psalm 23 resides here.[7] The rod with which he would typically lead and guide his sheep has become an instrument of harm (3:1). Instead of protecting the flock from dark places where they could get lost or attacked, the speaker claims he has "driven . . . me into darkness without any light" (3:2). A good shepherd protects the unsuspecting animals from predators, but here, the shepherd actually poses as a bear and again as a lion, ready to prey on the unprotected flock (3:10). Instead of leading them on a straight path, this tender of the

5. For example, the first lament ends in v. 20 but breaks the threefold acrostic unit 19-21 where each line begins with the Hebrew letter ז, *zayin*. Instead, v. 21 introduces a message of hope, the focus of the next unit, vv. 21-24.

6. This rendering is in contrast to the NRSV, which translates this phrase simply as "I am the one. . . ." (3:1).

7. Hillers (*Lamentations*, 124) suggests that the image in vv. 1-9 is a reversal of the shepherd in Ps 23. Berlin (*Lamentations*, 86) argues that all of vv. 1-13 are "constructed on the metaphor of a sheep and shepherd."

Lamentations 3:1-20

³:¹I am one who has seen affliction
   under the rod of God's wrath;
²he has driven and brought me
   into darkness without any light;
³against me alone he turns his hand,
   again and again, all day long.

⁴He has made my flesh and my
   skin waste away,
   and broken my bones;
⁵he has besieged and enveloped me
   with bitterness and tribulation;
⁶he has made me sit in darkness
   like the dead of long ago.

⁷He has walled me about so that I
   cannot escape;
   he has put heavy chains on me;
⁸though I call and cry for help,
   he shuts out my prayer;
⁹he has blocked my ways with
      hewn stones,
   he has made my paths crooked.

¹⁰He is a bear lying in wait for me,
   a lion in hiding;
¹¹he led me off my way and tore
   me to pieces;
   he has made me desolate;

flock only pretends to make them safe. He fashions crooked paths for them to follow, putting the sheep at risk (3:9).

Next, militaristic language describes further attacks by this assailant on the strong man. He becomes the target for this unnamed attacker's archery and is shot through by bow and arrow (3:13). Finally, the assailant shames and taunts the strong man (3:14). As if pushing the strong man's face to the ground, the assailant overpowers the victim, making him grind his teeth on gravel and cower in ashes (3:16). This violence is inflicted repeatedly: "against me alone he turns his hand, again and again, all day long" (3:3). The Hebrew word for hand (יד) also translates as power. Thus, the assailant's dominance is relentless against its victim. Throughout the description, no name is given to this torturer. The assailant remains unidentified, just as the attacker that Jacob wrestled throughout the night in his experience at the Jabbok (Gen 32:22-32). Unlike Jacob, however, the victim being attacked in this poem gives no indication that he fights back. Instead, despite his self-identification as the strong man, we hear only that he is physically annihilated, socially isolated, and spiritually debased.

Physically, the strong man describes himself as ravaged and perhaps even starved. With his flesh and skin wasting away, his frail bones are also crushed (Lam 3:4). He sketches an image of himself as walled in, but not in a protective sense (3:7). Instead, he describes a kind of captivity where he can be easily cornered and attacked. Any possible escape from

¹²he bent his bow and set me
   as a mark for his arrow.

¹³He shot into my vitals
   the arrows of his quiver;
¹⁴I have become the laughingstock
   of all my people,
   the object of their taunt-songs
      all day long.
¹⁵He has filled me with bitterness,
   he has sated me with wormwood.

¹⁶He has made my teeth grind on
   gravel,

and made me cower in ashes;
¹⁷my soul is bereft of peace;
   I have forgotten what
      happiness is;
¹⁸so I say, "Gone is my glory,
   and all that I had hoped for
      from the LORD."

¹⁹The thought of my affliction and
      my homelessness
   is wormwood and gall!
²⁰My soul continually thinks of it
   and is bowed down within me.

such an imprisonment has been blocked with hewn stones (3:9). Moreover, his confinement is secured with heavy chains (3:7). He describes this besieged state as one of "bitterness and tribulation" (3:5). He likens himself to prey for a wild animal that is waiting to destroy him. So similar is his experience to that of a plundered victim in the wilderness, he cries out that he has been torn to pieces (3:11). The experience renders him desolate and unable to protect himself. As if exposed and more vulnerable than ever, an arrow rips his vitals (3:13). Having succumbed to defeat, he partakes in only bitterness and wormwood. Wormwood, an exceedingly bitter herb, has sated him (3:15). Thus, it is no surprise that he becomes the bitterness that he has consumed.

Such a devastating physical assault gives way to social isolation. When he is walled in, he is alone in the dark. When he is led off and torn to pieces, no one witnesses this abduction or tries to rescue him. Attacked and defeated, he acknowledges that he has become "a laughingstock" and an "object of taunt-songs" (3:14). He is target for insults in his defeated brokenness. No one responds to his suffering. He is his only witness.

The strong man teeters on spiritual demise. Even his efforts to pray are ineffectual. He reports having tried to cry out in prayer, but his plea is shut out by the prison that walls him in (3:8). He himself admits that his soul, his very life, "is bereft of peace" (3:17). We hear him sink to the depths of despair. He cannot think beyond his current circumstances. When the Lord is finally mentioned by name (3:18), what becomes clear is that the strong man has been talking about God all along. God was the one who assaulted him, shamed him, isolated him, and brought him to this breaking point. That this man suffers a loss of hope is no surprise. Now that everything familiar is destroyed, he is fixated on his pain and his lack of place. He describes this experience of affliction and homelessness with the images of two very bitter herbs, wormwood and gall (3:19). His soul is bowed down deep within him (3:20). No one is present to hear him. His sorry state is a solitary state. No one is there to lift up his face.

A Faith That Denies Human Experience? (Lam 3:21-24)

The tone and theme of the strong man's recitations in 3:21-24 make so radical a shift from what has just preceded as to fuel skepticism about the motive and authenticity. From the depths of his theological despondency, he suddenly declares his utter faith in the mercies and kindness of God. This staggering declaration, "therefore I have hope" (3:21, 24), serves as the opening and closing framework featuring this unexplainable shift in disposition. In form, 3:21 belongs to the acrostic group 3:19-21, narrating the futility that precedes this section. But in content, this verse shares the optimistic outlook expressed in what follows. This disruption of the stanza ruptures the rigid order of the intense acrostic. The literary fracture might be heard as the upheaval and fragmentation in thought that permeates one so muddled in the chaos of suffering. With his soul bowed down so low, the strong man resorts to a theological sustenance from the past as balm for the intolerable conditions of the present. Even the order of his language bears evidence of this spiritual bedlam. In the concluding verse to what has come before, the "this" of "this I call to mind" (3:21) would logically imply he is referring to all the torture and travail he has just narrated in 3:1-20.[8] In the second half of the verse, "therefore" anticipates a consequence to his narration that has just identified God's active role in perpetrating all his anguish, but instead, the strong man does an about-face for which no reader or believer can be prepared. God, in whom all hope has vanished for the strong man (3:18), is now "therefore" the source of his hope. Some offer a literary explanation for this abrupt change, noting that such shifts in content are

---

8. Though the NRSV opens v. 21 with "but," this contrastive particle is absent in the MT, allowing the simple declarative statement "This I call to mind, and therefore I have hope."

Lamentations 3:21-24

²¹But this I call to mind,
and therefore I have hope:

²²The steadfast love of the LORD
never ceases,
his mercies never come to an
end;

²³they are new every morning;
great is your faithfulness.

²⁴"The LORD is my portion," says
my soul,
"therefore I will hope in him."

typical of laments,[9] but such illogical mood swings may also be heard as the internal struggles of one so mired in excruciating suffering. To miss the spiritual perplexity narrated by this shift risks bypassing the disclosure about the acute interior unrest accompanying deep human suffering offered here.

In the first part of the lament (3:1-20), the strong man narrates his experience of torment and brutality and eventually holds God responsible. In what follows (3:21-24), he resorts to his inherited theological tradition of a loving compassionate God as a lifeline amid his intolerable circumstances, but his narrated experience and his theology stand at odds with one another. His theology from the past is grounded in covenantal images of God. Despite his torment, this theological digression calls to mind God's steadfast love, that divine attribute recalling God's covenantal fidelity.[10] The prophets who persisted in reviving the people's fervor for covenantal fidelity frequently reminded them of the enduring feature of God's (חסד) "steadfast love" (Hos 2:21; Mic 7:18, 20; Isa 54:8, 10; Jer 3:12; 9:23; 16:5; 31:3; 32:18; 33:11). The strong man also recalls God's mercies, an outpouring in excess that often occurred as an elaboration of God's love (Exod 34:6; Isa 54:8, 10; 63:7; Jer 16:5; Hos 2:21; Zech 7:9). Finally, his emphasis on God's faithfulness holds familiar echoes of the people's deliverance as prayerfully reminisced throughout the psalms (Ps 36:5; 40:11; 88:12; 89:2-3, 9, 50; 92:3; 98:3; 100:5). In light of the strong man's experience thus far, however, the matter of God's covenantal fidelity becomes complicated.

In Lamentations 1 and 2, the scope and degree of Woman Zion's suffering is eventually deemed excessive on the part of the observer. Even

9. O'Connor, *Lamentations*, 49; Dianne Bergant, *Lamentations*, AOTC (Nashville: Abingdon, 2003), 90.
10. House, *Lamentations*, 414.

Woman Zion herself finally confronts God; she admits no guilt and accuses God of unwarranted violence (Lam 2:20-22). Furthermore, just prior to the strong man's outpouring of hopefulness in God's compassion and mercies, he himself describes his experience of being hunted, torn apart, and driven to the brink of utter desolation. Though his declaration of despair in 3:18 suggests the Lord as the one behind this suffering, nowhere does he hint that some iniquity on his own part warranted this barrage of painful punishment. The excess of God's violent assault in the experience of the strong man raises no questions yet about the very matter of God's covenantal fidelity, but unmitigated suffering (3:1-20) will eventually rupture denial and bump up against the limits of one's theological traditions and assertions (3:21-24). Suffering not only has costly physical and social consequences but also summons reexamination of one's beliefs with unpredictable spiritual consequences for those who have strength enough to dare.

The Hope of the Battered Women (Lam 3:19-22)

It is suitable to read Lamentations 3:19-22 in the context of Vietnam's culture, especially for the Vietnamese women. Though we are living in the twenty-first century with economic development and globalization and an emphasis on human dignity, Vietnamese women are still suffering multiple forms of oppression, discrimination, and exploitation in their own families and in society. As director of a female refuge hostel for young women between the ages of fifteen and twenty-two, I have regular direct contact with these young women and their mothers. The young female residents all come from poor, uneducated, and often broken families. Some are abused by their fathers, most of whom are drunkards or gamblers. Others have been subject to domestic violence by their husbands. The men in their lives are jobless and force these young women to work in order to earn money for their alcoholism and addictions.

A sixteen-year-old girl told me, "I want to go to school but my father forced me to drop out. He forces me to work in order to earn money for him. I am nearsighted, so my mother bought eyeglasses for me so I can keep studying. Every time she buys them for me, my father breaks them. He has broken my eyeglasses more than ten times. He even tears up my books and does not allow me to attend school. Sometimes, I hide my books in order to keep studying but when he finds out, he destroys my books, breaks my eyeglasses, and even hits me."

Another girl, who was called away from our group meeting,

returned to me crying. She blurted out through her tears, "My father was drunk and smashed furniture and then set the house on fire. My mom has to stay with my neighbors."

Another day a mother came to visit her daughter at the hostel. Her face was full of bruises and lacerations. I asked what happened. She tearfully replied, "My husband was drunk and battered both me and my children last night."

These women have no voice. They are unprotected and they have no sense of their self-worth. Yet still they are very religious women. They all confess to praying frequently. I struggle when I think about them praying but being so unprotected. Perhaps prayer becomes a safe refuge where they can give voice to their pain and despair, express their anger, and maybe even find hope amid their despair. Perhaps prayer is the only time they allow themselves to imagine a life beyond the current impasses where "The steadfast love of the LORD never ceases; God's mercies never come to an end" (Lam 3:22).

Sr. Anna Pham Phuc

The Contours of Hope

The shift in voice in Lamentations 3:21 jolts me. The poet has just dug deeper and deeper into the pit of despair, piling image upon image of physical agony, when suddenly there is a voice that utters: "I have hope" (3:21b). From where does this hope come? Is it a forced hope? A hope that one feels they should speak? In my grappling with this voice, I am reminded of a prayer circle I once participated in at a women's federal prison while doing ministry work there. In one of my first meetings, I remember feeling completely helpless when a woman unveiled her utter anguish. The day prior she had received a phone call with the stark news that her longtime boyfriend had just died. As if the news were not heartwrenching enough, she also was told that he had been seriously ill for quite some time but kept it all hidden out of fear of causing her more hardship. As she spoke, her pain became palpable and tears streamed down her face. Suddenly, I could tell she had been crying much of the night and day. She expressed the confusion and disorientation the present situation was causing for her, expressed the agony of not knowing where her boyfriend went after death, why this happened, and what it all meant. Then voices broke out from others in the circle as fellow inmates began to speak. While they affirmed her tears, they responded with expressions of hope, of God's providence and master plan. To hear words of such hope jarred me. I wanted to stay with the lament. I wanted to speak the words written earlier in chapter 3 of Lamentations: "Gone is . . . all I had hoped for from the LORD" (3:18). For me, it was the first time I ever considered that people in prison are often unable to say a final good-bye to their loved ones. The lack of closure this woman would now live with tore at my insides. All I saw was another place where dignity had been stripped away from this woman, leaving her more vulnerable than before. After the prayer meeting, I checked in with the woman to see how she was doing. While briefly lifted up by the prayer meeting, understandably, she was back in a state of dismay. Much like the continuing tone of Lamentations, the brief moment of hope was now gone.

When I think back on this time, about those voices of hope and the way they juxtaposed her cry, I am left wondering many things. Was the hope distant and removed? Fabricated or out of place? Were the statements shared by the group simply intellectual ideas about God, and thus detached from the pain of the woman grieving in the wake of losing her lover? Or maybe those are all simply my judgments. Maybe they did indeed give the woman a sense of solace, even if ever so brief. Maybe they were able to speak to her of a God she once believed in, or wanted to believe in but could not when all else was falling away. And maybe that was momentary relief. I do not know. But what I do know is that perhaps those women who sat around her in that prayer circle knew much more about how to hope in God than I ever will. It makes me wonder just how many women have sat next to their fellow inmates when they received news of death from "the outside" and have had to hold the other some way. While words of hope can feel fabricated at times, and ideas about God's goodness can appear far from the present reality, perhaps it is also true that uttering some drop of hope in a sea of despair is connected to a sense of dignity and resilience.

Sara Prendergast

Attempted Reconciliation Creates an Untenable Theology (Lam 3:25-39)

Immediately following the confession of hope, a theological reflection commences in which the strong man embarks on an attempt at reconciliation between his beliefs and his experience. As if trying to find meaning in the midst of suffering, he begins by enumerating what is good. First, he lifts up the Lord as good, especially for those who wait (3:25). Then he

Lamentations 3:25-39

²⁵The L̘ord is good to those who
    wait for him,
    to the soul that seeks him.
²⁶It is good that one should wait
    quietly
    for the salvation of the L̘ord.
²⁷It is good for one to bear
    the yoke in youth,
²⁸to sit alone in silence
    when the Lord has imposed it,
²⁹to put one's mouth to the dust
    (there may yet be hope),
³⁰to give one's cheek to the smiter,
    and be filled with insults.

³¹For the Lord will not
    reject forever.
³²Although he causes grief, he will
    have compassion
    according to the abundance of
    his steadfast love;
³³for he does not willingly afflict

or grieve anyone.

³⁴When all the prisoners of the
    land
    are crushed under foot,
³⁵when human rights are
    perverted
    in the presence of the Most
    High,
³⁶when one's case is subverted
    —does the Lord not see it?

³⁷Who can command and have it
    done,
    if the Lord has not ordained it?
³⁸Is it not from the mouth of the
    Most High
    that good and bad come?
³⁹Why should any who draw
    breath complain
    about the punishment of their
    sins?

adds that even waiting is good, when it comes to waiting for God's salvation (3:26). Finally, he sees good even when the waiting is encumbered by the burden of suffering. He uses the image of one bearing "the yoke in youth" to narrate this encumbrance (3:27). While his narration is seemingly impersonal, this image may be an indirect reference to himself, but because his own waiting in suffering has not been good, he lapses into a digression. His own experience prompts consideration of how waiting is also burdensome. A verbal triptych elaborates what is so difficult about waiting. First, "to sit alone in silence" he notes as problematic, especially if the Lord has ordained it. Such isolation sounds markedly similar to the dark walled-in circumstances he described earlier (3:2-8). Next he warns that "to put one's mouth to the dust" may be required while waiting (3:29). Again, this humiliating sign of complete self-abasement parallels the abuse the strong man himself reported having undergone earlier (3:16). Third and last, he suggests that waiting might even necessitate enduring bodily harm and accepting insults. This admission also sounds glaringly similar to his earlier outcries after incurring physical attacks (3:11-33) and then being made a laughingstock (3:14). The strong man works hard to establish the connecting thread between that which he views as good and the actual circumstances he has suffered, but the argument he puts forward is precarious. He himself straddles a thin tightrope stretched between an objective theology that seeds hope in God on one side and his own experience of pain and shame at the hand of God on the other.

A theological reflection on the three "goods" (3:25-27) moves the strong man beyond the pessimistic space of his anguish, but it also leads him to consider three conditions that could inflict suffering on those who wait for the good (3:28-30). Having detailed the conditions within which one might have to wait for God, the strong man now turns his attention to three reasons to trust in God for those who wait. First, he asserts that God will not turn away forever (3:31). O'Connor notes that this verse might be heard as the centerpiece of the whole acrostic, "occurring in the stanza at the alphabetic midpoint of the whole poem."[11] As focal point for the entire lament, however, this verse seems to indict the sufferer and exonerate God. Therefore, it narrates the contradiction of the man's faulty theology. Second, he alleges that though God has caused the grief, those who suffer will be met with an outpouring of divine love (3:32). Again the strong man resorts to covenantal language to elaborate his theology. God's compassion is grounded in חסד, that steadfast love promised in covenant. Finally, he claims that God does not cause suffering unwillingly (3:33). Renkema concurs, contending that it is against divine essence to afflict.[12] Hence, such suffering can be only the product of just punishment, but the notion of affliction by the divine as punishment stands in tension with the strong man's own experience. In fact, he has never suggested or admitted any wrongdoing on his part. Still, his struggle to renew his faith in God leads only to the worn-out impasse. The existence of suffering points blame at humans and renders God blameless. Pain and suffering bear association with God only in circumstances where the divine hand is forced against humans. That God might afflict unwillingly raises questions about the very nature of God. Does the divine not have control over the divine self?

11. O'Connor, *Lamentations*, 51.
12. Johan Renkema, *Lamentations*, trans. Brian Doyle, HCOT (Leuven: Peeters, 1998), 409–10.

Before the Most High

The strong man's inner reflection leads him deeper into theological uncertainty regarding God's actions. Setting aside circumstances when humans are unfaithful, he considers the plight of the innocent whom others have harmed (3:34-36). In Hebrew, each of these three verses begins with an infinitive (לדכא להטות לעות), as if what follow are products of a wandering train of thought that complicate his previous certainties. First, he considers the plight of all the prisoners of the land crushed under oppression. Next, he shifts to circumstances where human rights are violated. Here he notes that all of this happens in full view of the divine, "in the presence of the Most High" (3:35). This assertion already anticipates the question with which he will conclude in 3:36. Finally, he cites the instance when an individual's lawsuit is undercut. As all of these examples narrate injustice against innocent parties, he wonders, "Does God not see?" (3:36b). Framed as a rhetorical question, the strong man assures himself that indeed God does look and know. Heard as a genuine inquiry, he continues his theological probing as to the very nature of God.

Throughout Lamentations 1 and 2, God's attention had been repeatedly summoned (1:9c, 11c, 20a; 2:20a), but no response had been forthcoming. The strong man himself asserts that when he cried for help, even his prayer was shut out (3:8). So he now rivets his attention directly on God and the divine nature (3:37-39). With a rhetorical question, he asserts God's all-powerfulness over everything that happens (3:37), but behind this affirmation of such omnipotence must lodge his own inner query of why God does not rescue him. He probes further, but whether his next consideration asks another rhetorical question or makes a declarative statement remains an uncertainty in the translation of the Hebrew. "Is it [It is] not from the mouth of the Most High that good and bad come" (3:38)? Perhaps the grammatical uncertainty contributes to the ambiguity surrounding his waning confidence in what he really knows about God. Do both good and evil come from the Lord as consequence of human actions, or are they the unpredictable product of divine whim? Does evil really originate with God? All this inquiry seems to lead the strong man further into a discomforting abyss. Hence, with his final question he settles back into his inherited theological tradition even at the expense of denying his own experience. Deuteronomy and the revivalism of the prophets make clear that suffering issues from breaches of covenant. Thus, if one is still breathing and has life, even in the midst of well-deserved punishment, why should he question and why should he complain (3:39)? All this was ordained from the beginning.

A Communal Return to God (Lam 3:40-42)

The resolution that the strong man finds at the end of all this soul searching (3:25-39) causes a shift in address to take place. He gives up his introspection and turns to what must be his community. Armed with a theological conclusion (3:39) that compromises and even denies his own experience, the strong man enlists others to participate in a prayer of confession with him. Using first-person plural address, he speaks directly to the community, inviting them to conduct a self-examination as the necessary prelude for their "return to the LORD" (3:40). His summons then becomes communal prayer: "Let us lift up our hearts as well as our hands to God in heaven" (3:41). By directing both the interior disposition, symbolized with reference to "our hearts," and the external self, signified by reference to "our hands," he invites their complete submission to God. Praying with them and on their behalf, he implies for the first time his own sinfulness. Yet there is no counterpart to this confession in his previous recitation.[13]

Still, an uplifting tone of hope permeates the recitation. A longstanding Deuteronomic theology ensures that suffering followed by repentance yields God's forgiveness.[14] Hence, on the heels of their confession—"We have transgressed and rebelled" (3:42a)—a well-grounded expectation of God's gracious mercy and rescue builds. But like a thunderbolt without warning, the strong man proclaims that no divine clemency is forthcoming. In the hearing of the community, he speaks directly to God and charges that "you have not forgiven" (3:42b). In a moment, hope again is ruptured and the stage is set for the lament that follows.

Indictment against God (Lam 3:43-66)

The abruptly aborted call to communal confession, repentance, and supplication now becomes a caustic affront to God. The strong man accuses God of blanketing the community with divine anger (3:43). In contrast to his earlier assertion of the Lord's unceasing love, he directly charges God with not only pursuing them but killing them without pity (3:43). The indictment undercuts and perhaps even negates the strong

---

13. Carleen R. Mandolfo, *Daughter Zion Talks Back to the Prophets: A Dialogic Theology of the Book of Lamentations*, SemeiaSt 58 (Atlanta: SBL Press, 2007), 73.

14. Miriam J. Bier, *'Perhaps There Is Hope': Reading Lamentations as a Polyphony of Pain, Penitence, and Protest*, LHBOTS (New York: Bloomsbury T&T Clark, 2015), 127.

Lamentations 3:40-42

⁴⁰Let us test and examine our ways,
　　and return to the Lᴏʀᴅ.
⁴¹Let us lift up our hearts as well
　　as our hands

to God in heaven.
⁴²We have transgressed and
　　rebelled,
and you have not forgiven.

man's earlier confident proclamation in divine mercies that never cease (3:22). Instead, the very character of God is in question. The strong man's description charges that the Lord rejected their efforts to return, nullified their attempts to repent, and rebuffed their overtures to seek forgiveness. All supplication, as well as the pleas for forgiveness of the community, has been thwarted. The longstanding theology no longer holds. Berlin views this as possibly the most disturbing idea not only in the chapter but in the entire book.[15] Apparently, whether or not forgiveness will follow repentance remains uncertain. Moreover, the strong man charges that God is not even accessible. With a stinging reproach, he describes God as having blocked all human access to the divine with a cloud (3:44). The image of cloud is particularly poignant as it was associated with divine guidance in the exodus and the manifestation of God's presence at Sinai (Exod 13:21; 14:19-24; 16:10; 19:16; 33:9-10). The cloud was one of the fundamental symbols by which God's abiding presence protected the people. Now the cloud has become the barrier blockading all their prayerful overtures to the God who could save them. More significant, it denies them access to the divine presence. Since the earliest traditions, the promise of God's presence was the fundamental notion inscribed in all the theological traditions. From the covenant to the prophets, the promise of the divine presence would be the mainstay of those who remained faithful and those who were called to be God's intermediaries. The notion of being walled off from God's presence creates a most troubling theological impasse. "Nowhere in Lamentations and perhaps in the entire Bible is God's refusal to be present more strongly expressed."[16] This spiritual blockade denies the people access to their one source of hope and identity amid despair and ruin. The consequences of this denial take on historic proportions. The people called by God to be the channel through which all nations would be blessed (Gen 12:3) have not only

15. Berlin, *Lamentations*, 96.
16. Ibid.

Lamentations 3:43-66

⁴³You have wrapped yourself with
   anger and pursued us,
   killing without pity;
⁴⁴you have wrapped yourself with
   a cloud
   so that no prayer can pass
   through.
⁴⁵You have made us filth and rubbish
   among the peoples.

⁴⁶All our enemies
   have opened their mouths
   against us;
⁴⁷panic and pitfall have come
   upon us,
   devastation and destruction.
⁴⁸My eyes flow with rivers of tears
   because of the destruction of
   my people.

⁴⁹My eyes will flow without
   ceasing,
   without respite,
⁵⁰until the LORD from heaven
   looks down and sees.
⁵¹My eyes cause me grief
   at the fate of all the young
   women in my city.

⁵²Those who were my enemies
   without cause
   have hunted me like a bird;
⁵³they flung me alive into a pit
   and hurled stones on me;
⁵⁴water closed over my head;
   I said, "I am lost."

⁵⁵I called on your name, O LORD,
   from the depths of the pit;

been cut off from the divine presence; they have been rendered by God as "filth and rubbish among the peoples" (Lam 3:45).

Eyes That Bear Witness to Horror and Absence

Attention now shifts from the absence of God to the presence of enemies. The pervasiveness of the catastrophe and its consequences are lodged in the language. A parade of vivid references—"enemies with opened mouths," "panic," "pitfall," "devastation," and "destruction" (3:46-47)—all testify to the atmosphere of trauma. The strong man's repeated narration of his own tears (3:48, 49, 51) in the face of the destruction echoes Woman Zion's account of her tears at the shattering of her city (2:2, 16). Almost as a condition of waiting, he reiterates that his tears flow without stopping in an attempt to coax God to look and see (3:50a). Again, the desire to have God gaze and behold such human pain recalls Woman Zion's summons for God to see (1:9c, 11c, 20a; 2:20a). In one of the most cherished traditions (Exod 2:23-25), God's hearing, remembering, and seeing the people's suffering under Egyptian bondage resulted in the divine intervention that became the exodus. This heritage suggests that the empathic nature of God would be so moved by the sight and

⁵⁶you heard my plea, "Do not
  close your ear
  to my cry for help, but give me
    relief!"
⁵⁷You came near when I called on
  you;
  you said, "Do not fear!"

⁵⁸You have taken up my cause,
  O Lord,
  you have redeemed my life.
⁵⁹You have seen the wrong done
  to me, O Lᴏʀᴅ;
  judge my cause.
⁶⁰You have seen all their malice,
  all their plots against me.

⁶¹You have heard their taunts,
  O Lᴏʀᴅ,

all their plots against me.
⁶²The whispers and murmurs of
  my assailants
  are against me all day long.
⁶³Whether they sit or rise—see,
  I am the object of their taunt-
    songs.

⁶⁴Pay them back for their deeds,
  O Lᴏʀᴅ,
  according to the work of their
    hands!
⁶⁵Give them anguish of heart;
  your curse be on them!
⁶⁶Pursue them in anger and
  destroy them
  from under the Lᴏʀᴅ's
    heavens.

cry of human pain and that divine mercies and compassion would follow. Thus, the strong man continues to try to attract divine attention by making reference to his own eyes that have seen the suffering all around (Lam 3:51). He explains that these sights have been the source of grief as they bear evidence of the horror and its aftermath. Specifically, he mourns the fate of all the young women of his city (3:51). The dreadful fate of young women in wartime at the hands of the enemy was always violent and invasive. Again and again, women were victims of molestation and sexual slavery as consequence of military conflict between men. Little has changed in human history.

Finally, the strong man turns again to his own experience (3:52-54). Indirectly asserting his own innocence, he charges that enemies have made him a victim without cause. Enlisting the metaphor used earlier in his outcry, he describes himself as being hunted like a bird (3:52). Reminiscent of his ancestor Joseph who was thrown in a cistern as well as Jeremiah who suffered similar treatment, he tells of being "flung into a pit" (3:53). This entrapment is made worse when stones are hurled upon him. His description of the experience sketches an image of one being buried alive. To ensure his death, water fills the tomb-like encasement in which he is enclosed. As the water rises over his head, he cries out—much like Jonah from the depths of this abyss—"I am lost" (3:54).

The Chains Revealed within a Prison

"He has walled me about so that I cannot escape; he has put heavy chains on me; though I call and cry for help, he shuts out my prayer; he has blocked my ways with hewn stones, he has made my paths crooked." (Lam 3:7-9)

Amy was addicted to heroin at a young age, primarily influenced by her parents who also struggled with addiction. The walls of poverty, and the lack of education and adult support did not allow for her to escape a life intoxicated by drugs and violence. The chains of addiction and of being a woman kept her down and vulnerable for violation.

Jess always comes off as a lighthearted and kind person. Only once has she hinted at some past gang activity. Most of her efforts are directed toward battling depression while trying to deal with the losses from her past. She has been on suicide watch at least twice since I have known her. Mental illness makes the darkness of prison confinement even more burdensome.

April was always willing to share but nothing was directly about her own experiences. She had been a drug dealer until, one day, an underaged teen died from April's drug transaction. Now, walls of guilt and regret trap her from a sense of self-love and self-worth.

These three women and many like them will be forever without escape. These verses in Lamentations record again the cries of the imprisoned—this time, women in prison who have been walled in, chained up, and shut out even before being incarcerated. Now in the physicality of the prison, they experience shame, humiliation, and abuse while being physically confined and enclosed in a cubicle of brick and mortar. It is disheartening to know that many of them will continue to be isolated, walled in, and never really free even after their release.

Kelly Miguens

Characteristic of the mood swings and alterations in outlook occurring across this poem, the strong man calls on God for rescue immediately after declaring he is lost. The text here poses a challenge for translators and interpreters alike. Different verb tenses alternate across these verses, leaving uncertainty as to whether the speaker is addressing what God has done in the past or expressing a wish for what he hopes that God may do in the present.[17] But thus far in Lamentations, God has not acted, been

17. Philip Graham Ryken (*Jeremiah and Lamentations: From Sorrow to Hope*, Preaching the Word [Wheaton, IL: Crossway, 2001], 758), Robin A. Parry (*Lamentations*, THOTC

heard from, or been seen, despite the pleas uttered. In addition, 3:55-66 are most frequently understood to be part of the appeal to God for rescue. Therefore, instead of translating these verbs as narrating past events, Bier considers reading these verbs as perfects so that "3:55-66 . . . be understood as an entreaty for help from within the midst of suffering."[18]

A God Who Punishes or a God Who Rescues?

This unexpected entreaty to God appears grounded in a puzzling confidence. With all his vacillation between hope and despair as well as his accusations against God, the strong man's resort to the Lord from "the depths of the pit" is inexplicable.[19] Such an about-face stands in stark contrast to Woman's Zion's response at the end of Lamentations 2. Though urged to cry out, repent, and offer supplication to the God who was identified as the source of her demise (2:18-19), she flatly refused. She confronted that theology with boldness and honesty, and ultimately rejected it. With unmitigated strength, she arose from her victim status, and named the God of that theology the abuser and enemy of human integrity (2:20-22).

By contrast, the so-called strong man cultivates a spirituality predicated on a theology that sacrifices his self-worth. The God who he claimed had broken his bones and enveloped him with bitterness (3:4-5) is now the one to whom he turns for relief. The failure of God to see does not dissuade him from confidently beckoning God to hear (3:56). Though he accused God of blocking off all access by a cloud, he now claims that God is near (3:57). He even anticipates God speaking words of comfort, urging "do not fear" (3:57). Yet nowhere in Lamentations does God ever utter words of consolation or make any response to a human plea.

Then, as if God needs to be reminded, the strong man recites all that he has unjustly endured at the hands of his enemies (3:58-63). He recalls the taunt-songs, plots against his life, and wrongdoing that his assailants

---

[Grand Rapids: Eerdmans, 2010], 124), House (426), and Robert B. Salters (*Lamentations: A Critical and Exegetical Commentary*, ICC [New York: T&T Clark, 1994], 266) read the verbs as past perfects narrating what God has done in the past. Thus far, however, Lamentations narrates that God has not heard or responded, which justify reading these verbs as precative perfects. See Hillers, *Lamentations*, 74; Iain Provan, *Lamentations*, New Century Bible Commentary (Grand Rapids: Eerdmans, 1991), 105–9; Archie Chi Chung Lee, "Mothers Bewailing: Reading Lamentations," in *Her Master's Tools? Feminist and Postcolonial Engagements of Historical-Critical Discourse*, ed. Caroline Vander Stichele and Todd C. Penner, GPBS 9 (Atlanta: SBL Press, 2005), 208.

18. Bier, *'Perhaps There Is Hope,'* 132.

19. O'Connor, *Lamentations*, 55–56.

have conjured "all day long." This action sets the stage for his final request before the Lord (3:64-66). Aware of God's anger and its potential to destroy (3:43), he asks that God now "pursue them in anger and destroy them" (3:66). He summons a kind of vengeance from God that he himself has experienced. Then he urges that it be directed at those who have made him suffer. He requests that the Lord punish these enemies whom the strong man now holds responsible for his own plight (3:64-65).

Contradictions abound in the strong man's final oration. The God who has so besieged him is now, in the last resort, a reliable source of rescue and retaliation. The Holy One who was wrapped in hot anger and who killed without pity will be the one to provide relief. The Lord who disowned the covenant community, leaving them to be considered as "rubbish" among the peoples, will fight against their enemies. A theology so at odds with the strong man's experiences may be the result of wishful thinking. Or it may just stem from the delirium and confusion that invades the human spirit when rendered so fragile by intolerable suffering. Or it may be the product of denial on the part of one who once thought himself strong and powerful but has now been rendered weak and powerless.

Lamentations 4

"Life Drains Away"
(Lam 4:9c)

A Hunger for Hope

Returning to the opening of chapters 1 and 2, Lamentations 4 also begins with איכה ("How"). The now familiar acrostic form also fashions the framework of the poem with each letter of the Hebrew alphabet introducing the first of the two lines of each stanza. While the verses are longer than those in chapter 3, they are shorter than those of the first two poems. The abbreviated form anticipates and coincides with reductions narrated in the poem. Hope is almost nonexistent; there is staggering lack of food and the already diminished well-being of the people has declined further.[1]

Two speakers are heard in chapter 4 and their speaking parts delineate a structure. The predominant speaker comes across as a detached observer. No evidence supports the point that he needs to be identified with the observer in chapters 1 and 2. His tightly contained report sets forth some of the most disturbing and graphic images of the siege. His

---

1. Kathleen M. O'Connor, *Lamentations and Tears of the World* (Maryknoll, NY: Orbis Books, 2002), 58.

tone, however, is emotionless and impersonal. While this tone could be perceived as the product of his objective stance, it could also be the result of burnout. Emotional numbness and exhaustion could be expected given all the atrocities that he has witnessed. A communal voice constitutes the second speaker. In their collective recitation, they too recount their experience of the siege and its devastating consequences. Unlike the previous instances where the community has raised their voice, this communal recitation never cries out for rescue from the Lord. The only hope they express is for their enemies to receive the same fate that they have encountered in the destruction. Hence, the structure of the poem can be ordered according to the speaking parts. In 4:1-10, the observer narrates the ongoing human carnage during the siege and points a blaming finger at women of Zion. In verses 11-16, he continues this blame game and now holds religious and political officials responsible. The second half of the poem features the community. First, they witness to their experience of these unfoldings (Lam 4:17-20). In the closing verses (Lam 4:21-22), the community finds the strength only to hope that their enemy will suffer as they have suffered.

Blessings of the Covenant Become Human Carnage (Lam 4:1-10)

With the opening exclamation "How" the lone observer may be mourning the loss of valuable gold and precious stones now littering the streets after the destruction (Lam 4:1), but the second stanza makes clear that he is fixed on the human carnage, in particular the fate of children. This unfathomable loss almost defies narration. The "precious children of Zion, worth their weight in fine gold" (4:2a), are the treasures of the people. They are the gold and sacred stones that in the opening verses were symbolized as permanently altered because in real life, pure gold never fades. Hence, this image narrates a new circumstance of which no one has ever known. The image of "gold [that] has grown dim" bespeaks an unthinkable reality that they had never conceived.[2] Children who had always represented the future and the blessing of this covenant people are starving and dying. They are the impossibly tarnished gold and the randomly scattered sacred stones. That they lie "at the head of every street" (4:1) recalls previous images of the little ones "who faint for hunger at the head of every street" (Lam 2:19). It also summons a

---

2. F. W. Dobbs-Allsopp, *Lamentations*, IBC (Louisville: John Knox, 2002), 130.

4:1How the gold has grown dim,
   how the pure gold is changed!
The sacred stones lie scattered
   at the head of every street.

2The precious children of Zion,
   worth their weight in fine gold—
how they are reckoned as earthen
      pots,
   the work of a potter's hands!

3Even the jackals offer the breast
   and nurse their young,
but my people has become cruel,
   like the ostriches in the
      wilderness.

4The tongue of the infant sticks
   to the roof of its mouth for thirst;
the children beg for food,
   but no one gives them anything.

5Those who feasted on delicacies
   perish in the streets;
those who were brought up in purple
   cling to ash heaps.

6For the chastisement of my
      people has been greater
   than the punishment of Sodom,

which was overthrown in a moment,
   though no hand was laid on it.

7Her princes were purer than snow,
   whiter than milk;
their bodies were more ruddy than
      coral,
   their hair like sapphire.

8Now their visage is blacker than
      soot;
   they are not recognized in the
      streets.
Their skin has shriveled on their
      bones;
   it has become as dry as wood.

9Happier were those pierced by
      the sword
   than those pierced by hunger,
whose life drains away, deprived
   of the produce of the field.

10The hands of compassionate
      women
   have boiled their own children;
they became their food
   in the destruction of my
      people.

recollection of the earlier reference to the young men and women who lie dying in the streets (2:21). Now these emblems of a hopeful future are reckoned not only as having lost their value and worth; they have become as mere breakable earthen pots (4:2).

This severed destiny of the children is not tied specifically to the destruction of the city. Rather, women once again are indirectly held responsible. The image of jackals offering their breasts and being attentive to their young contrasts with mothers of Jerusalem not nursing their infants (4:3a). These mothers too are starving and unable to nurse their famished little ones. Still the failure of mothers to provide for their offspring is unthinkable. These starving mothers' dried up breasts will not absolve them. The observer calls this lack of response to starving children "cruel"

(4:3). He compares it to the behavior of ostriches in the wilderness that on occasion treat their offspring harshly and even abandon them (4:3). As he continues, the images that indict those who care for the young sketch even more graphic and horrific consequences. The thirsty infant with its tongue stuck to the roof of its mouth paints a disturbing picture of a dried up, dying, emaciated child (4:4a). The moaning whimpers of young ones are almost audible as the poem describes children begging for food to no response (4:4b) from the mothers who ordinarily nourish them.

Famine Does Not Discriminate

In times of famine, the social differences between adult and child, the wealthy and the poor, the servants and the royal class all collapse. The young are not the only ones who suffer from the lack of food; those accustomed to "feasting on delicacies" also starve (4:5a). Alongside dying children, these elite also perish in the street. Reference to those raised in the finery of purple clothing further identifies persons of means whose state is altered (4:5b).[3] Though once able to afford such colored clothing, they now live a destitute life. While not yet lying in the streets with others who have perished, they rummage through garbage heaps seeking the sustenance characteristic of the poor. The evidence in these public places, where young and old, rich and poor lie dying, testifies that everyone is affected.

No words can adequately describe the new reality or the cost to human lives as a result of this calamity. The observer resorts to the past in an effort to narrate what seems unreal. He compares the chastisement of Judah to the punishment of Sodom (4:6a). Sodom, along with Gomorrah, the archetypes of sinful corruption, was destroyed in an instant (Gen 19:23-25). While also punished for its failure in covenant, Jerusalem, by contrast, has encountered a prolonged siege and several stages of destruction. The comparison speaks to the incomparable sinfulness of the inhabitants of Jerusalem. Though recalling earlier times often prompted hope, the suffering survivors would hardly be comforted by such a comparison to Sodom.

Verses 7 and 8 also embark on a comparison but from the not-so-distant past. The initial description sketches the appearance of those representing the epitome of health and well-being in recent times. Jerusalem's princes displayed pure complexions, healthy bodies, and hair like sapphire (Lam 4:7). The reference to "hair like sapphire" suggests thick shining heads of

---

3. Dianne Bergant, *Lamentations*, AOTC (Nashville: Abingdon, 2003), 113.

hair characteristic of ones well groomed and in good health. By contrast, in verse 8 these emblematic portraits of a state of well-being are dashed. The complexion "whiter than milk" and bodies "more ruddy that coral" (4:7) have become blackened. Their soot-like appearance makes these distinct and familiar royal presences unrecognizable. More graphically, their skin has become "shriveled on their bones" (4:8). Suggestive of an emaciated physique, their skin likely appears pale, lacking elasticity, "dry as wood." The color and form that bespeaks vitality and life has been drained from these once vibrant bodies.

Lamentations 4 in the Tenderloin

In the Tenderloin, the poorest neighborhood of San Francisco, *jewels lie scattered at the corner of every street*, begging to be *worth their weight in gold*. The homeless women and men of this community are *treated like clay jugs, the work of any potter*. These children of God *beg for bread, but no one gives them a piece. Now their appearance is blacker than soot; they go unrecognized in the streets*. God, where are you? These are the miseries of a besieged city.

Besieged by what, or by whom? The poverty stricken in the Tenderloin primarily consists of immigrants, minority racial and LGBTQ populations, veterans, and individuals who are mentally ill. Systems of oppression perpetuate a hostile takeover of God's vulnerable people. Babylonian colonization destroyed the sacred temple of Jerusalem, just as sexism, homophobia, racism, and unfettered capitalism desacralize human worth in the Tenderloin. Similarly, patriarchal interpretations of the Bible too often distort and destroy the sacred temples that dwell within the powerless. Israel's

lament to the Lord resounds in feminist exegetical scholarship, which *lay[s] bare the sins of a society*, and a sacred history, that disempowers the "second sex" and nonnormative "others." Feminist interpretations of the sacred biblical text provide a message of hope for women and other marginalized populations: *the Lord will not prolong your exile*.

I tried to hand down this message to the poor and vulnerable of the Tenderloin while interning at a holistic health and healing center for addicted and homeless populations. I was facilitating spiritual life discussion groups at this center, striving to accompany those who were *pierced by hunger* for food and for God. *The Lord will not prolong your exile*, I ached to proclaim to the group, but my voice was often stifled by the realities of their suffering.

In one group I had planned to facilitate a discussion on the book of Lamentations and to subsequently invite participants to write their own laments to God. *The Lord will not prolong your exile*, I thought to myself, as I gave participants time to write their laments, but no one was writing. Several participants revealed their incapacity to lament because of the extent of their suffering. "I cannot write to God about the things that upset me," one participant expressed, "or I will unravel . . . and I have no one to take care of me if I were to reach that place of darkness. I know this from experience." Many participants agreed with this sentiment. Their suffering and depression were so intense, and their sense of community so lacking, that it was dangerous for them to express grave laments. We live in a society in which its most vulnerable members do not feel safe enough or loved enough to lament or grieve their suffering. They fear that expressions of pain will leave them too dysfunctional and vulnerable in unsafe shelters and on violent streets, especially given that they do not receive proper care for their various illnesses.

God, where are you? Why are things not otherwise? Fifty years ago, in his book *The Triumph of the Therapeutic: Uses of Faith after Freud*, sociologist Philip Rieff warned that the psychological person was replacing the religious person, as demonstrated by the decline of the value of religious tradition and community, especially in Western cultures. Rieff argues that the rise of the therapeutic process, and its emphasis on the quest for self-realization, shifts the locus of authority from religious or communal tradition to the self. In a therapeutic culture, Rieff suggests, morality is that which is "conducive to increased activity" such that "the important thing is to keep going." Rieff believes that while the religious person was born to be saved, the psychological person is born to be pleased. His words are prophetic in light of Lamentations 4 and the reality of our inability to weep. Must we "keep going" when so many people are suffering? Inclusive feminist activism and biblical scholarship must continue to cultivate tenderness, critical analysis, and hope. *Even now our eyes are worn out, searching in vain for help. From our watchtower we have watched for a nation unable to save.* Lord, please do not prolong our exile.

Kathleen Cooney

As he takes in a view of the aftermath of the siege, the observer offers some concluding observations (4:9-10). From the famished children wandering the street to the royal young officials no longer recognizable, the impact of the food stress has redrawn this community's portrait. In light of the enemy assault and the subsequent famine, death is not a question. It cannot be avoided. If any hope can be conjured in these circumstances, it is the hope to die quickly. A rapid death by an attacking sword is far preferable to the long, protracted experience of "those pierced by hunger" (4:9). "Deprived of the produce of the field" (4:9), one gradually becomes physically weak, mentally distraught, and spiritually depleted. It also requires that one cope with the growing awareness that "life drains away" due to starvation and that there is nothing that can be done to avert it.

Women: Victimized and Indicted

Almost as an afterthought, the observer adds that death by starvation has led to even more unspeakable circumstances. Mothers have boiled their own children for food in an effort to address their hunger (4:10). Ironically, he refers to these women as "compassionate," a word derived from the Hebrew root רחם, meaning "womb," the adjectival form of which is used only with reference to the Lord in the biblical tradition (Exod 34:6; Deut 4:31; Joel 2:13; Jonah 4:2; Pss 78:38; 86:15; 103:8; 111:4; 145:8; Neh 9:17, 31; 2 Chr 30:9). The use of the term could intend sarcasm at women's expense, or the reference to "compassionate" might suggest a laudable though pathetic motive to which desperate mothers resort in order to curtail children's prolonged suffering. Finally, the description of "compassionate mothers" boiling and eating their children may serve to narrate the drastic social change that has invaded the lives of the community.[4] Mothers, once compassionate, have now become cannibalizing mothers. In any case, the impact is the same. Women symbolize the moral desperation that has invaded the community in these incredibly hopeless circumstances. The curse in Deuteronomy 28:53-57 addressed in the second-person plural to the whole community is also likely being echoed here. It warned that in wartime, men and women would eat the flesh of their offspring if Israel violated the covenant, but in verse 10, the portrait charges only compassionate mothers with the curse. Hence, once again, women, like Woman Zion in chapters 1 and 2, become the scapegoat representing both the iniquity and its dreadful consequences.

In fact, the account of cannibalism here does not serve to indict mothers but points the accusing finger elsewhere. Cannibalism as tied to hunger is far more complex than simple cause and effect. Rather, its existence is yoked to a prevailing sociopolitical structure of hierarchy and domination. Cannibalism or its absence is not the direct consequence of food

---

4. Phyllis Trible, *God and the Rhetoric of Sexuality*, OBT (Philadelphia: Fortress, 1978), 33, suggests that these women were formerly compassionate but have lost their capacity to feel compassion.

stress but specifically associated with the prevailing ethos of a society.[5] Where accommodation and harmony are subordinate to or replaced by domination and control, cannibalism may constitute a response to famine. The patriarchal society that featured kings and royal advisors, cultic officials and prophets, military leaders and heads of households made up that hierarchy of domination and control. But they are nowhere in sight when the description of moral decay or the horrific consequences are tallied here. Women consuming their children are not the accomplices of the violence that has visited this society. Women and their children are the powerless ones being consumed by the waywardness of powerful men dominating the community.[6] Hence, women's loss of their maternal instinct serves as the exponent of the degree of moral decay stemming from a hierarchical society that made them victims.

The Pathos of Choice

Is it possible to read the entire book of Lamentations without finding a speck of hope, until focusing on the verse that seems the most appalling? "The hands of compassionate women have boiled their own children; they became their food in the destruction of my people" (Lam 4:10). I read that verse at least four times before seeing and hearing the word "compassionate," the word that encompasses, expresses, and engenders hope.

Suddenly, seeing that these are compassionate women, they became for me not cruel, not heartless and selfish, not greedy, self-serving women feeding themselves at the expense of their children. (I had wondered if in similar desperate circumstances I would do the same.) Able to focus on their compassion, I could see them as women caught in the horror of a torturous time, whose lives had become unimaginably altered by war, who faced destruction, loss, and famine, and whose

---

5. For an extended study of cannibalism as tied to the prevailing ethos of a cultural system, see Peggy Reeves Sanday, *Divine Hunger: Cannibalism as a Cultural System* (Cambridge: Cambridge University Press, 1986). For a study of the practice and significance of cannibalism as related to particular cultures, see the collection of essays in Paula Brown and Donald F. Tuzin, eds., *The Ethnography of Cannibalism* (Washington, DC: Society for Psychological Anthropology, 1983).

6. So also the study on cannibalism in 2 Kings 6:20-31 in Gina Hens-Piazza, "Forms of Violence and the Violence of Forms: Two Cannibal Mothers before a King (2 Kings 6:24-33)," *JFSR* 14 (1998): 91–104.

children had perished. I pictured them sitting on the ground in mourning rocking their emaciated babies, soothing their dying infants. The pathos of their choice on how to proceed in wartime, how to live in the misery of defeat, how to survive your own child's death as you yourself slowly starve to death sets forth an excruciating example of the depths of human suffering. The ravages of war then and today comprehensively redefine everything—survival, motherhood, and even compassion.

Mary Olowin

The Force of Divine Rage (Lam 4:11-16)

Now the observer turns attention away from the human cost to his explanation of how and why this happened. God's rage is first identified as the cause of dehumanizing chaos (4:11). With three images—wrath, anger, and fire—he emphasizes the consuming nature of the divine response. Moreover, he qualifies God's wrath as being delivered with "full vent" (4:11a). Nothing partial about the destruction can be conjured. The fire in Zion consumed even its very foundations (4:11). Such stone work was not ordinarily subject to destruction by fire. But the divine fire manifests a reality unfamiliar to humans. Like the potential of the divine fire that fell from heaven on Carmel and consumed the bull, the wood, and even the stones in the Elijah tradition (1 Kgs 18:38), the very foundations of Zion are destroyed in this inferno.

No one could believe what they heard or what they saw. Like other ancient cities built on the high places, Jerusalem presided as a well-fortified center high on a hilltop. Its walls, gates, and urban structures were visible from afar. With the temple in view, a belief reigned as to the city's inherent sacredness (Pss 2; 9; 14; 20; 48; 50; 132; 135) due to the abiding presence of God in its midst (Pss 46:3; 48:1-3).[7] That "kings of earth did not believe" (Lam 4:12) that Zion's security could be compromised is, however, likely an exaggeration expressing the observer's own incredulity. Still, not difficult to imagine is that those inhabitants from the surrounding region were startled when the city's well-fortified gates had succumbed to enemy attacks (4:12). The gradual realization that the impossible had happened urges once again the neuralgic question "Why?"

Having joined the other voices naming Yahweh as the principle cause for Jerusalem's destruction (1:5-6, 12c-15, 17b; 2:1-8, 17, 20-22; 3:1-18,

---

7. Bergant, *Lamentations*, 116.

Lamentations 4:11-16

¹¹The Lord gave full vent to his wrath;
    he poured out his hot anger,
and kindled a fire in Zion
    that consumed its foundations.

¹²The kings of earth did not believe,
    nor did any of the inhabitants
        of the world,
that foe or enemy could enter
    the gates of Jerusalem.

¹³It was for the sins of her prophets
    and the iniquities of her priests,
who shed the blood of the righteous
    in the midst of her.

¹⁴Blindly they wandered through
    the streets,

so defiled with blood
that no one was able
    to touch their garments.

¹⁵"Away! Unclean!" people
    shouted at them;
    "Away! Away! Do not touch!"
So they became fugitives and
    wanderers;
    it was said among the nations,
    "They shall stay here no longer."

¹⁶The Lord himself has scattered
    them,
    he will regard them no more;
no honor was shown to the priests,
    no favor to the elders.

43-45), the observer now seeks to pin down a more concrete perpetrator of the divine wrath. Priests and prophets were the mediators of the divine will and presence to the community. For their sins, the whole community now suffers. They are even accused of shedding the blood of the righteous.Though not intended to suggest these religious leaders literally participated in the actual slaughtering of their people, the metaphoric message is clear. Those appointed to lead the way to God are the wayward ones responsible for the divine punishment resulting in the shedding of innocent blood (4:13). Thus, prophets, the seers who conveyed God's will to the people, ironically have become the blind wandering the streets (4:14). Priests, responsible to observe purification regulations so as to perform rituals of cult, have become the defiled whom no one must touch. Ironically, the religious officials who made God's will and presence accessible to the people are now themselves inaccessible. The community suffers because the deeds of their religious leaders deceived them. No one can come in contact with them. Unlike the lepers who go about the streets warning people that they are unclean, the people in the streets shout out warnings regarding these religious leaders (4:15). They have become the contaminated ones. This constitutes a profound reversal. Those who were the heart of the community conveying God's presence to the people have become the fugitives and wander at its periphery. As if alienation from the community were not enough, the observer notes a further severing that isolates priests and prophets.

Not only do the people distance themselves from the prophet and priest, but God "will regard them [these religious officials] no more" (4:16). The Holy One who anointed them is described as disowning these religious men. All respect and honor due such leaders has been forever erased. They retain no identity or status now that the divine providence has turned away from them.

A Weary Community Speaks (Lam 4:17-20)

For the first time, that the observer has been speaking to a community now becomes clear. With first-person plural speech, the people of the now destroyed city raise their voice and witness what they experienced. Up until now, they have only spoken about the horrible conditions of the aftermath. Now they give voice to the actual experience of the enemy invasion.

In contrast to the many references of weeping eyes, they speak of weary eyes (4:17). Their reference to failing vision suggests the exhausting hours of watchfulness as the enemy approaches and begins to enter the city. These are not yet eyes of grief and weeping. Instead, efforts to secure safety command the people's vigilance. As they see the enemy enter the city, they look for help from "a nation that could not save" (4:17b). Whether the Hebrew לֹא יוֹשִׁעַ yields "could not save" or "would not save" remains unclear. Hence, Egypt may be implicated here as the "nation that would not save" because Egypt was an archenemy of Babylon, but a reference later in the poem suggests Edom as the nation "that could not save" before a military power like Babylon. Whether or not a neighboring nation refused or was unable to come to the rescue of Judah remains insignificant. The rescue for which the people watched with weary eyes failed to materialize.

The siege was so daunting and terrifying that the people could not appear in public (4:18). They could not venture out in the streets where they might find help. They could not go to public places where supplies still available for survival could be acquired. They could not be seen in the streets trying to escape. The terror that gripped the community in those initial hours of panic and confusion begins to dawn. Here it is given a threefold iteration: "Our end drew near; our days were numbered; for our end had come" (4:18).

For those who dared to attempt escape, the enemy's pursuit was swift. The community's witness compares these hostile warriors to eagles

Lamentations 4:17-20

¹⁷Our eyes failed, ever watching
   vainly for help;
we were watching eagerly
   for a nation that could not save.

¹⁸They dogged our steps
   so that we could not walk in
   our streets;
our end drew near; our days were
   numbered;
   for our end had come.

¹⁹Our pursuers were swifter

than the eagles in the heavens;
they chased us on the mountains,
   they lay in wait for us in the
      wilderness.

²⁰The Lord's anointed, the breath
      of our life,
   was taken in their pits—
the one of whom we said, "Under
      his shadow
   we shall live among the
      nations."

who characteristically hover over areas in searching for desperate prey hiding in the thicket (4:19). In a moment and without mercy, they swoop down and plunder what life remains. No place provided hiding for these hunted. Whether fleeing to the mountains or hiding out in the wilderness, the attackers painstakingly tracked those who attempted escape (4:19).

Nothing, however, can compare to the shockwaves that rippled through the city when the king, "the Lord's anointed," was captured (4:20). That he was their "breath of life" narrates his significance as more than sovereign governor. In the covenantal history, the king acted as the vice-regent for God. His office guaranteed protection under divine providence. His presence and office signified the very life of the people. The promise that David's heir would always be on the throne must have remained a glowing ember even amid the assault. But now their captured ruler was taken and put in enemy prison. The king under whose shadow they would always find safety "was taken in their [the enemy] pits" (4:20). As the Zion theology collapsed, the community succumbed to despair and contemplated their fate. Whether in hiding, captured, or scattered among the nations, they would live under the shadow of their imprisoned king.

The Cup Passes, Another Woman Falls Victim (Lam 4:21-22)

For the first time in this poem, a shift to second-person address occurs. Yet, God, the typical addressee of the people is bypassed. Instead, their message is unexpectedly aimed at Edom. As twin brother of Jacob, Edom shared an ancestral past with his sibling. Though traditionally descen-

Lamentations 4:21-22

²¹Rejoice and be glad, O daughter Edom,
you that live in the land of Uz;
but to you also the cup shall pass;
you shall become drunk and strip yourself bare.

²²The punishment of your iniquity,

O daughter Zion, is accomplished,
he will keep you in exile no longer;
but your iniquity, O daughter Edom, he will punish,
he will uncover your sins.

dants of the same family, Edom often played the part of the stereotypical enemy of Judah (Isa 34:5-17; 63:1-6; Ezek 25:12-14; 35:3-15; Joel 4:19; Mal 1:2-5).[8] Geographically, Edom was situated east of the Jordan, with Israel as its southwestern neighbor.

The surviving chorus summons Edom to "Rejoice and be glad" (Lam 4:21). They address their geographic neighbor as "daughter Edom," suggesting their call is directed to the capital city of Edom, but immediately their seemingly gracious overture discloses their seething mockery. Edom is going to be brought low and shamed. Given the perpetrator of destruction and siege, Babylon, rather than Edom, would be the expected target of such venom. Perhaps Edom had an opportunity to come to Jerusalem's rescue during the siege and refused. Though not identifying Edom specifically, the people recalled that despite their desperate expectation for rescue from a nation, no help arrived (4:17). Because of the longstanding hostility with this neighbor (Obadiah; Ps 137:7; Ezek 25:12-14), Edom may merely be code for enemy nations.[9]

The "cup" that will pass to Edom (Lam 4:21b) that will be her shame is the traditional "cup of the wine of wrath" (Jer 25:15) that the prophet was to deliver to Jerusalem and its surrounding towns. Eventually, it would also be provided to all the surrounding nations. While drinking cups of wine would ordinarily be a sign of merriment and celebration, this cup was different. This one was the cup of wine from which an excess would cause drunkenness and stupor. "They shall drink and stagger and go out of their minds because of the sword that I am sending

8. John R. Bartlett, *Edom and the Edomites*, JSOTSup 77 (Sheffield: Sheffield Academic, 1989), 151–61.

9. Francis Landy, "Lamentations," in *The Literary Guide to the Bible*, ed. Robert Alter and Frank Kermode (Cambridge, MA: Belknap Press, 1987), 333–34.

among them" (Jer 25:16). This drink would be a toxin that would result in their humiliation. Thus, the cup became a symbol of the outpouring of a divine wrath (Isa 51:17, 22; Jer 25:15, 17, 28; 51:7; Ezek 23:31-33; Hab 2:16; Ps 75:9) as punishment for their sin. Partaking of this cup, Edom will become so intoxicated that she will strip herself bare. Again, like Woman Zion, Edom's nakedness will be her shame, and again, like woman Zion, this exposure of her nakedness anticipates the public disclosure of Edom's sins.[10]

Despite the degrading nature of their kinship, Daughter Edom is informed she will change places with Daughter Zion. Edom will endure destruction and decline while Jerusalem experiences restoration and return (Lam 4:22). Other than the fleeting hope expressed by the strong man (Lam 3:22-24), the reference to Judah's punishment being complete is viewed by some scholars as the only real hopeful verse of the entire book.[11] This thin expression of hope, however, not only comes at Edom's expense but also takes on again the metaphoric form of another woman's body and its shaming debasement.

Invitation to Lament

How many times must a woman's body be enlisted to evoke shame and indignity on behalf of a people and their iniquity? Why must the exposure of a woman's nakedness serve as poetic trope to disclose the reality of a whole community's sinfulness? The frequency with which this image occurs in the tradition warrants both suspicion and objection. The narration of Daughter Edom's and Woman Zion's nakedness, along with the rape and dismembering of the Levite's concubine (Judg 19:1-30), the defilement of Tamar (2 Sam 13:1-22), the abduction of the maidens of Shiloh (Judg 21:20-23), and all the other biblical texts of terror narrate a litany of evidence documenting women's enduring reality. Such traditions not only summon evaluation and critique to their role in Sacred Scripture but also invite *lament*. Therefore, when women pray Lamentations, this gesture is not just one of mourning; it becomes an act of dissent that documents and denounces these degradations.

For those outside the grip of comprehensive loss and suffering, the desire for vengeance toward Edom seems like a deplorable closure to the people's recitation. That they make public their wish for Edom to suffer

---

10. Robin A. Parry, *Lamentations*, THOTC (Grand Rapids: Eerdmans, 2010), 143.
11. Delbert R. Hillers, *Lamentations*, AB 7A (Garden City, NY: Doubleday, 1992), 91.

as they have suffered comes across as ruthless. Yet, laments are intended to provide emotional as well as personal agency. They make way for the most honest outpourings of the human heart. They open a space where harbored feelings, thoughts of revenge, and angry sentiments can be vented. In genuine laments, there are no filters as to what is admissible and what cannot be said.[12] These recitations offer an occasion where suffering humanity can give voice to their greatest strengths and their most reprehensible brokenness. All the sentiments that can potentially warp the human psyche or further embitter the wounded spirit find an avenue for exit in lament.

As this fourth poem comes to its conclusion, it ends with this address to Daughter Edom and to Daughter Zion. This appearance of Daughter Edom is the only one in these poems. This is the last time Woman Zion appears in the entire book of Lamentations. Though she is spoken to, she is denied speech in this final appearance. "As an act of violence, this is absolute. The subsuming of the individual in the communal, and the silencing of the Woman is complete."[13] Her voice as metaphoric woman is absorbed into the community voice that becomes the only speaker in the upcoming and final poem in chapter 5. Though she has borne both the iniquity as well as the punishment of this community, her silence and subsequent absence constitute her erasure. When women who have suffered violent abuse go unrecognized, are denied speech, and eventually are disappeared, violence is licensed to rear its head again.

---

12. See Gina Hens-Piazza, "Learning to Curse: Catharsis, Confession, and Communion in the Psalms," *Review for Religious* 53 (Winter 1994): 860–65, for a discussion of catharsis as a boundless scope as to what is admissible in laments.

13. Miriam J. Bier, *'Perhaps There Is Hope': Reading Lamentations as a Polyphony of Pain, Penitence, and Protest*, LHBOTS (New York: Bloomsbury T&T Clark, 2015), 162.

Lamentations 5

"Why, O LORD, Have You Forgotten Us?" (Lam 5:20)

Lifting the Veil of Human Suffering

Unlike the preceding four poems, Lamentations 5 opens and closes with direct address to the Lord (Lam 5:1, 21-22). These calls to God form a perimeter within which the poetic oration unfolds. More than another disclosure of the suffering of survivors, the address to God situates this recitation in the context of a prayer. As sentiments of grief, desolation, and hopelessness have multiplied across the first four chapters, these brackets of direct address create the only boundaries within which this final climactic outpouring can be contained. Even the acrostic structure that gave order to the chaos disclosed across the earlier accounts has been all but abandoned here. The twenty-two lines that parallel the number of letters of the Hebrew alphabet are the sole indicator of a structural connection. As the suffering persists, it grows more intense. Thus, the absence of the acrostic "signifies the abandonment of efforts to contain the suffering within a recognizable alphabetic order."[1]

---

1. Kathleen M. O'Connor, *Lamentations and the Tears of the World* (Maryknoll, NY: Orbis Books, 2002), 71.

The shortest of the poems, the fifth chapter's abbreviated length mirrors the survivors' dwindling stamina occasioned by prolonged unaddressed suffering. As if the product of their diminishing energy, the verses in Lamentations 5 are shorter and, for the most part, abandon the *qinah* rhythm.[2] Like classic Hebrew poetry, fairly balanced parallelism shapes most of the brief two-line stanzas throughout. As if over time the repetitive narrations of suffering have become stunted, the parallelisms fashioning these verses have a staccato-like character. The clipped tenor of these recitations conveys the faltering spirit of those still struggling to survive.

The collective outcry resounding in this poem defines the final speaker of the book. With first-person plural speech, the chapter most closely resembles the format of the communal lament.[3] Three parts of this liturgical genre structure the content that unfolds. First, the poem opens with a direct address to God (5:1). Next, a three-part complaint follows (5:2-18). The complaint comprises most of the poem. Finally, a petition for God's deliverance from the affliction closes the lament (5:19-22). Glaringly absent, however, is the final characteristic recitation of praise that often concludes laments and anticipates with confidence the divine response. Such an omission echoes the accelerating despair that accumulates across this prayer. While the people desperately turn to God again in this more formal lament, their words convey a diminished conviction that God will respond, correlating with the unending desperation that reaches a zenith in this poem. As the final chapter to a book that testifies to the grief, anguish, and confusion brought on by the destruction of Jerusalem, this poem neither offers resolution to the suffering nor provides answers to the questions with which survivors wrestle. Instead, its communal voice augments and reinforces the painful accounts of the individual voices in Lamentations 1–4. The collective testimony here amplifies the anguish that resonates throughout this book. It erupts with an array of emotions, tries on a variety of theological viewpoints, and reflects fragmented thought processes. Rather than offering an acceptable closure to such difficult accounts, this final poem concludes with a deepening of hopelessness. Instead of fashioning some satisfying explanation for what has occurred, it affords an unadulterated close-up with survivors and their anguish. Hence, while it does not provide answers, the final chapter does lift the veil on the experience of human suffering.

---

2. F. W. Dobbs-Allsopp, *Lamentations*, IBC (Louisville: John Knox, 2002), 144, notes, however, the *qinah* in Lam 5:2, 3, and 14.

3. Dianne Bergant, *Lamentations*, AOTC (Nashville: Abingdon, 2003), 125–26.

A Communal Voice Summons Divine Attention (Lam 5:1)

Characteristic of the lament (Pss 44, 60, 74, 79, 80), this last poem opens with a direct address to God. With three imperatives—"remember," "look," and "see"—the communal voice summons divine attention (Lam 5:1). The earlier image of God as walled off from prayer by a cloud (Lam 3:44) may explain this emphatic iterative overture. Those making the plea do not request remembrance of the earlier days of promise and covenant; instead, they ask God to call to mind the recent disgrace that has befallen them. They seek more than recollection. The word "remember" requests that God call to mind that which will motivate action in conjunction with the remembered devastation. The recent suffering, however, brought about by destruction and siege, is not the only focus; the people plead with God to "look" and "see" them now as they struggle to survive. Though the address to God is about the present, it faintly echoes the earliest days of their sacred tradition. Under the harsh conditions of Egyptian slave masters and even before this people knew the divine presence, God knew them. God called to mind their suffering, remembered the covenant with the ancestors, and knew (Exod 2:23-25).

Though Woman Zion has not been heard from since the end of the second lament (Lam 2:20-22), the insistence of the people's address here imitates the directness of her closing response to the Lord. Like the community, the brave city woman also called on God to "look." She boldly summoned God to "look" specifically, however, at what divine recklessness had brought about. By contrast, the people's request retreats from lashing out at God. Their lack of confidence amid their suffering causes them to simply bid God observe their disgrace. They level no suggestion that the divine hand may have had any part in this catastrophe. Woman Zion's prayer complained about the pain and degradation God's actions had brought upon the community. The community, however—depleted and perhaps uncertain about their relationship with God—complain only about their circumstances. These descriptions sketch them as the faltering survivors left behind in the land of Judah now ruled by foreigners.

Following the direct address, the complaint (5:2-18) comprises the second portion of the lament and catalogues the community's grievances along three lines. Verses 2-10 report the psychological and physical hardships. A second section (5:11-14) illuminates the social and personal degradations that have become commonplace. Finally, citation of the sentiments and symbols that defined meaning as they once knew it registers among the losses (5:15-18).

Lamentations 5:1

5:1Remember, O Lord, what has
befallen us;
look and see our disgrace!

Psychological and Physical Hardship (Lam 5:2-10)

The first round of grievances laments the forfeiture of the people's inheritances (5:2). The reference to inheritance (נחלה) carries the meaning of ancestral lands as well as individual family land tracts, but more is lost here than territorial possession or agricultural fields. Israel's religious and cultural identity was tied to the gift of the land. This ancestral inheritance bound them to a past (Lev 25:25-28; Num 27:8-11; 1 Kgs 21:14). Being deprived of this inheritance equates to much more than a financial or even political loss. The gift of land, which defined them as a people in conjunction with this deity, has now been turned over to strangers (Lam 5:2).

This loss of land coincides with the social disintegration of the family once tied to that inheritance. The extended families that defined the clans and tribes of Israel's lineages constituted the basic unit of cooperative living on the land. The loss of land, coupled with the losses in wartime, dismantles this key social unit. References to themselves now as "orphans," "fatherless," and "widows," mothers attest to the collapse of this familial integrity (5:3). The loss of the father, carried off into exile or killed in battle, leaves women and their children displaced victims in a patrilineal society. In a time of enemy occupation, when socioeconomic safeguards no longer existed, women and children became particularly vulnerable. Hence, the anxiety surrounding the question of identity is intensified, soon to be replaced by a concern for survival.

A Weakened, Weary People

Preoccupations in life have become fixed upon the most elemental concerns. The basic commodities of water and wood are no longer free or even readily available (5:4). The yoke on their necks (5:5) may refer symbolically to their sense of being enslaved by these conditions or literally to the weight of having to carry daily staples long distances. The

²Our inheritance has been turned
over to strangers,
our homes to aliens.
³We have become orphans,
fatherless;
our mothers are like widows.
⁴We must pay for the water we
drink;
the wood we get must be
bought.
⁵With a yoke on our necks we are
hard driven;
we are weary, we are given no
rest.
⁶We have made a pact with Egypt
and Assyria,
to get enough bread.
⁷Our ancestors sinned; they are
no more,
and we bear their iniquities.
⁸Slaves rule over us;
there is no one to deliver us
from their hand.
⁹We get our bread at the peril of
our lives,
because of the sword in the
wilderness.
¹⁰Our skin is black as an oven
from the scorching heat of
famine.

heaviness of these physical loads, whether symbolic or actual, gives way to a psychological weightiness. Their cries of "we are hard driven," "we are weary," and "we are given no rest" (5:5) paint a painful triptych of a people collapsing under such burdens.

Even food must be procured at a price. Bread, the nourishment that sustains the life of the body as well as the livelihood of the community, was purchased with a pact in the past (5:6). The community acknowledges the fallacy of foreign alliances that, at the time, guaranteed to make them secure (5:6). Assyria, which is no longer a power by the time of the Babylonian exile, likely represents Mesopotamia in the East, while Egypt symbolizes the empire in the West. Hence, this familiar pairing of Assyria and Egypt suggests the geographical scope from east to west where Israel in previous times sought foreign kinship to secure its well-being. The Hebrew translation of "have given a hand to Egypt and Assyria" clarifies the exact cost. "Hand" (יד) often means "power." Symbolizing foreign nations from one end of the Fertile Crescent to the other, these two nations represent the scope of foreign engagements with which Israel sought protection in the form of alliances and vassalships. The prophets warned that such dependencies—trusting in foreign powers rather than trusting in God—would eventually contribute to their downfall (Isa 27:13; Hos 9:3; 11:5; Zech 10:10-11).

Echoes from the Post-Soviet Era

> *Our inheritance has been*
> *turned over to strangers,*
> *our homes to aliens.*
> *We have become orphans,*
> *fatherless; our mothers are*
> *like widows. (Lam 5:2-3)*

These verses of the final chapter of the book of Lamentations deplore the aftermath of the foreign military invasion that resulted in the capture of the holy city. Such destruction has striking parallels in the not-too-distant history of those nations that were part of the Soviet Union until 1991. The power vacuum and corruption, created not only by the fall of the empire but also by the disintegration of the particular Soviet mentality, allowed injustice to reign on macro- and micro-levels of the social life. Lamentably, those mostly struck by these circumstances were the most vulnerable social groups: single women and widows, orphans, retired people. . . .

Svetlana Alexievich, the Nobel Prize laureate in literature in 2015, has gathered in her book *Secondhand Time* the stories told in the first person by many women and men who lived in the grim conditions of the post-Soviet era.

Yulia, one of Alexievich's interlocutors, shares a tragic story of her family from Moscow. The story involves three women—her grandmother, her mother Ludmila, and herself, a fourteen-year-old girl at the time. They were victims of the bandits that prospered in Russia in the beginning of the 1990s. The problems started with the grandmother's death: her pension, the only source of income for the family, had barely allowed them to survive. Unemployed, her daughter Ludmila could not even provide for an appropriate burial of her mother.

Unexpectedly, some strangers who seemed to have come from nowhere helped with the burial and brought them food and new clothes. They convinced Ludmila to sell her three-room apartment and buy a smaller one in order to have resources for living. Then another group of bandits appeared and ousted the previous gang. The bandits did not bother to negotiate and threatened Ludmila that she would never see her daughter again if she did not transfer the property rights for the apartment to them. Ludmila tried to resist but finally complied: there was no point in seeking protection with the corrupt police. Mother and daughter were given a ramshackle hut in a village a few hundred miles from Moscow in exchange for their apartment. They lived a few months there, but when winter came, they decided to move back to the capital; they would not have survived the winter in the hut. They lived in train stations together with thousands of other homeless people that streamed to the city from all over the ex–Soviet Union.

After many wanderings, Ludmila gradually became an alcoholic, and one day Yulia received the news that her mother, at the age of forty-seven, died under a train just outside Moscow. Ludmila felt crushed by the weight of her plight and lost all desire to live. From the orphanage, Yulia was picked up by Nadezhda, a single woman, whom she calls "my guardian angel." While living with Nadezhda in her 170-square-foot apartment, Yulia was diagnosed with disseminated sclerosis but also found love with the neighbor's nephew Zhenya. Now Yulia has a new desire to live. And she dreams of a home.

Retold by Victor Zhuk, SJ

The recall of past infidelities as explanation for present circumstances takes on a more explicit indictment in what follows. For the first time, the community acknowledges the role of sin as they grapple for an explanation for their suffering. The people allege, however, that the surrounding destruction and personal loss stem from the iniquity of the previous generation (Lam 5:7). The belief that children might pay for the sins of their ancestors is well attested, especially in the early traditions of the Hebrew Bible (Exod 20:5; 34:7; Deut 5:9; Lev 26:40; Num 14:18). That it was later contested so adamantly by prophets like Jeremiah and Ezekiel (Jer 31:29-31; Ezek 18:1-4) suggests its endurance as an explanation for suffering even at the time of the exile. The retributive justice embedded in this punitive system defined illness, loss of prosperity, conquest by an enemy, and other tragedies in life as punishment that could be visited not only on the one who sinned but also on subsequent generations. The description of misery that follows elaborates those punishments of this later generation within this experience of the Babylonian subjugation.

The community laments two clear deficits marking the experience of the post-siege occupation. The first, the anguish caused by the loss of self-governance (5:8), is surpassed only by the second, the scarcity of food and resulting threat of famine (5:9-10). Their cry that "Slaves rule over us" may suggest that those outsiders who once served the inhabitants of Judah are now in charge because they collaborated with the Babylonians. More likely, those "slaves" given jurisdiction over the remaining inhabitants of Jerusalem are lower-class citizens who served in Babylon (2 Kgs 25:24).[4] The insult of being ruled by these foreign

4. Iain Provan, *Lamentations*, New Century Bible Commentary (Grand Rapids: Eerdmans, 1991), 129.

servants is undoubtedly accompanied by other abusive practices of the occupation. Moreover, this upside-down social arrangement bears the sting of all that has changed. The people once ruled by the king who was the descendant of David are now ruled by the servants of a foreign king. Their king, meanwhile, is carried off to the foreign land where these new masters were once slaves. Indeed, as the survivors' cry makes clear, there is no one now to deliver them (5:8). But the need for political deliverance is overshadowed by more basic necessities. One has to put one's life on the line just to gain access to bread (5:9). It is unclear what defines the exact threat, but obtaining food now entails peril to self. A reference to the "sword in the wilderness" symbolizes the threat.

The "sword in the wilderness" is often understood to be a metaphoric reference to bandits or Bedouins who had to be defended against in vying for food.[5] Verse 6 suggests that food is scarce, which likely results in exorbitant food prices. The similarity in Hebrew, however, between the words for "sword" and "heat" (*hōreb* and *hereb*) could urge an emendation meaning the "heat of the wilderness" which puts all life in peril.[6] Verse 10 corroborates this connotation with both the image of skin "black as an oven" and with the explicit reference to the "scorching heat of famine." Famine's association with hot climates was well known in and around Judah. The Judean history documents numerous experiences of famine (Gen 12:10; 26:1; 47:1; Ruth 1:1-2; Sam 21:1; 2 Kgs 18:2). Those living in the wilderness-like dry climate of Judah itself knew all too well the devastating effects of unending heat without rain. The hot weather predisposed individual inhabitants to dehydration. The downturn in agricultural production also meant high prices in the marketplace and not enough food to go around. Hence, the effort to procure food in these circumstances became an activity that threatened the life that very nourishment intended to sustain. The community's lament over these physical and psychological strains suggests the burden shouldered by those left behind to survive after the exile. Drought and the concomitant threat of disease and starvation abound. The unaffordable prices for basic necessities along with the scarcity of food make daily tasks fixed on simply surviving. Finally, the utter humiliation of being controlled by those who were slaves in another society exacerbates these tangible hardships in the struggle to stay alive.

---

5. See reference to Thomas McDaniel, "Philological Studies in Lamentations," *Bib* 49 (1968): 51–52, cited in Adele Berlin, *Lamentations* (Louisville: Westminster John Knox, 2002), 121.

6. Berlin, *Lamentations*, 121.

Fate of Women in Wartime (Lam 5:11-14)

The second part of the complaint (Lam 5:11-14) discloses the dehumanization on both personal and societal levels as a result of being controlled by these outsiders. No one in their previous social identity remains unaffected. The tally of tribulations spotlights married and unmarried women, young and old men, princes and elders, and even young boys. The humiliation incurred by each of these social groups underscores the dismantling of the society's infrastructure as a whole. Young men who represented the future and brought the pleasure of music (5:14) to the community are now forced to grind (5:13). Their nimble fingers, whose melodies once contributed to the sense of harmony, are now being worn down turning the millstone in the gristmill. Boys stagger with the imbalance and burn of the heavy loads of wood they are required to carry. Though young, they bear weights as well as insults by doing the work of the pack animals (5:13). Princes, elders, and men with a history of notoriety are all demoted. Charged in the past with the responsibility for governance, they now endure particular dishonor. Princes, once powerful, have become utterly disabled. They are ignominiously strung up, perhaps in public view (5:12). Elders who once gave counsel and made judgments at the gate receive disqualification: "no respect is shown to the elders" (5:12b).

"Elders Have Left the City Gate, the Young Their Music" (5:14)

The survivors in Jerusalem grieve for both the old and the young, mentioned together. They lament the disintegration of communal life, the loss of the experienced guidance of the elders and of young people's joyous expressions that might direct and enliven the community for the future. Their wail echoes the young people with whom I work at a Catholic university. I hear the laments of students as they speak of being prepared for their professional and cultural lives yet feel utterly unprepared to address adequately the question of the Mystery of God. They have been deprived of "elders" of our own time who might have led them to tend to their interiority, their spiritual lives. They say their generation is overwhelmed and benumbed with a stream of sad and hard news, the constant barrage of information they see every day over the internet. "We feel we can do nothing," one student said. "It's almost cool, normal, to be cynical." "We live in an existential vacuum," said another student. The grief of the students I hear—their mourning and despair, their *laments*—are prayers of the distraught.

Just as the elders abandoned the gate, it seems many of the

parents of the young people I hear from did not want to "force religion" on their offspring and therefore left their children "to find their own way." Some students report, "By the time I was born, my parents were no longer practicing Catholics, so I was raised knowing that there was a God, but knew nothing about God."

Just as the elders abandoned the gate, teachers, priests, and pastors failed to listen deeply to the young; instead, those in authority often counseled the acceptance of unexamined belief and ritual. Hence, many students report they have rejected the distant, remote patriarchal figure of God, a remnant of the Modern Theism of the eighteenth and nineteenth centuries, yet they are left with no other way to speak of the Holy Mystery. Many students at age eighteen are self-identified atheists.

In one upper-division theology class, the discussion of Jesuit Teilhard de Chardin's *The Divine Milieu* prompted one student to remark, "This is the first time I've thought about my spirituality. Growing up Catholic you would have thought that would have been addressed, but not so." "We need some guidance, but have had to fend for ourselves," said one student. Another one added, "And we often make mistakes along the way."

Jean Molesky-Poz

Korean Comfort Women

As a Korean woman, "the rape of virgins" narrated in Lamentations rings uncomfortably familiar in my cultural heritage. I recall often hearing of a traumatic practice by the Japanese army during their colonial rule (1910–1945) of my country. They would choose young Korean girls as "comfort women." These young girls, some as young as fourteen, were forced into sexual servitude for the pleasure of Japanese soldiers before and during World War II. The trauma and horrors experienced by a large number of teenaged virgins has been well documented. The atrocities suffered by these young women rendered them infertile, injured, pregnant, and afflicted with sexually transmitted diseases. These sexual slaves were often assigned Japanese names, given Japanese uniforms, and assigned to "comfort stations" where they worked all day. If a young woman did not sufficiently please a soldier, she might be beaten. Later, when some of these abused women returned to their communities, they lived in shame and disgrace and suffered terrible post-traumatic stress disorders; many even committed suicide. When the passing reference to "Women are raped in Zion, virgins in the town of Judah" (Lam 5:11) is actually unpacked, the potential suffering that these women experienced is unspeakable.

Yoon Kyung Kim

¹¹Women are raped in Zion,
virgins in the towns of Judah.
¹²Princes are hung up by their
hands;
no respect is shown to the
elders.

¹³Young men are compelled to
grind,
and boys stagger under loads
of wood.
¹⁴The old men have left the city gate,
the young men their music.

Women's Trauma Goes Unrecognized

Finally, at the opening of this litany of citizens who now enjoin a destitute future (Lam 5:11-14), the fate of women receives poignant and indisputable documentation (5:11). The sexual violation of women during the siege now continues to afflict those left behind after exile. The Hebrew verb used here (עִנָּה) clearly intends to indicate rape. The reference to both women and virgins serves to clarify that all women, both married and unmarried, are targets. Further, the sexual degradation broadens its horizons beyond female residents of the plundered city. Not only in Zion but also "in the towns of Judah" (5:11), women are being assaulted.

In a patriarchal society, preying on women was a war tactic directed against the men to whom they belonged. Their violation by the enemy constituted a brazen act demonstrating military superiority. Often women were carried off in battle as spoils. Additionally, these captured women performed a further function in battle. As powerless captives, they were likely pressed into service and forced to satisfy the sexual appetites of enemy troops away from their homeland during times of duty. As groups of women were rounded up, they were exchanged between groups of men like possessions confiscated in wartime. Their sexual violation was intended to contaminate the ethnic or national purity of the conquered group from which they were taken. Moreover, the rape of mothers and daughters insulted the identity of a father and undermined the familial structure as backbone of the patriarchal household. Hence, while men were the intended target of this insult or revenge, sexually abused and violated women were the means to level this assault. The experience of these women, however, receives no narration. The physical harm, the psychological pain, and the personal humiliation that a woman endured during such abuse never receives exposition. Her trauma does not qualify as a worthy focus for elaboration. The rape and defilement of her person, whether by enemy troops or by the militia of her own country, enjoin no uproar or lament. Her pain and loss of virginity warrant no recognition.

In this final communal prayer, the fate of suffering women left behind after exile joins with that of their metaphoric mother, Woman Zion. The distinction between the female literary artifact in Lamentations 1 and 2 and the real women victims of Jerusalem and the surrounding towns begins to dissipate. They share a common destiny, acting as shields behind which men are safeguarded from both blame and punishment. Prophetic texts make clear that the king and his royal class of advisers, along with priests and other religious officials, governors, and merchants, bore major responsibility for the destruction that was promised if they did not mend their ways. In a patriarchal society, these offices were the prerogative of men. Hence, the corruption and decay of the society run by men stemmed from their failure to honor the covenant in their work. One must question how the destruction of Jerusalem—viewed as punishment for this iniquity—ends up tied to the metaphor of a woman, Daughter Zion. Yet "evading blame by hiding behind a woman's figure is nothing new."[7] Like Eve in the earliest tradition of the garden, Woman Zion is assigned responsibility and bears the blame for this central calamity, and the women and virgins of Jerusalem and its surroundings endure the violent punishment for this male mischief. Why in biblical literature do women, metaphoric and real, bear the blame and why are they dealt the punishment rather than the real male culprits responsible for the calamity and carnage?

Fatigued Spirits (Lam 5:15-18)

The final section of the complaint component captures the loss of meaning that once infused life in Jerusalem and the surrounding region. The first-person plural address echoes the community collectively witnessing the loss of the meaning and vitality they once knew. That joy has ceased to enliven their hearts (5:15a) suggests the deflated disposition with which they now endure. These fatigued spirits no longer participate in dancing they once knew. That such festive activities have been replaced by mourning (5:15) discloses the absence of the delight and gladness of the past. They lament that the crown has fallen from their heads (5:16). The image not only suggests the loss of honor and self-rule but also indicates a state of disregard and disgrace (Job 19:9). The

---

7. Deryn Guest, "Hiding Behind the Naked Women in Lamentations: A Recriminative Response," *BibInt* 7 (1999), 413.

Lamentations 5:15-18

¹⁵The joy of our hearts has
ceased;
our dancing has been turned
to mourning.
¹⁶The crown has fallen from our
head;
woe to us, for we have sinned!

¹⁷Because of this our hearts are
sick,
because of these things our
eyes have grown dim:
¹⁸because of Mount Zion, which
lies desolate;
jackals prowl over it.

confidence in who they once were has been all but extinguished. This admission of mounting lifelessness and growing despair yields to an admission of sin: "Woe to us, for we have sinned" (Lam 5:16b). Unlike verse 7, which locates an explanation for the calamity in the past generation's sinfulness, here the community blurts out their own claim of responsibility for what has occurred. Some interpretations work to collapse these two different notions of sinfulness into a unified explanation. Others suggest that because this is a communal lament, different positions that exist in the community regarding who is responsible are embedded in this prayer. Some point to the ancestors' iniquity, while others call to mind their own guilt. It is also possible, however, to read this vacillation between two explanations for the destruction and its aftermath as the complex dynamism of a profound suffering. The questions of how and why plague the sufferer, who wavers between self-blame and desperate attempts to identify other explanations. Yet, in the face of suffering, no explanation is completely adequate. In the midst of prolonged anguish, one contemplates a variety of reasons, grapples with losses, and wrestles the disquiet, only to come up short of any satisfying answer at all.

With the possibility that they are being punished for their own sins, verses 17-18 detail what might be read as the unsettling consequences. The people's capacity to feel and see has been sorely compromised. Their hearts have become "sick" and their eyes have "grown dim" (5:17). But these alterations in sight and sentiment may also be interpreted as the community's experiences read forward "because of Mount Zion, which lies desolate" (5:18a). The people's vision has become compromised, and they are heartsick because of the devastation of their home, Zion. Finally, the closing image of jackals lurking about Zion and ready to plunder magnifies the people's regret (5:18b). It also summons, once again, the frequent real and metaphoric images of women plundered that emerge throughout this text.

A Community Summons God (Lam 5:19-22)

The community's prayer now shifts from a complaint about their circumstances to a request directed toward God. The unusual syntax that opens verse 19 with the pronoun "you" draws attention to the specificity with which they make their final appeal. The "you" summons God's attention, leaving no question as to whom this closing petition is directed. Calling on God in such a straightforward manner conveys a determination that their appeal not be missed. They begin with a statement of praise; that God's throne endures becomes a theological assertion (5:19). No longer thought to be confined to the temple, which has been destroyed, the divine throne takes on a more cosmological character. God's presence, which was once thought limited to Zion, now eclipses the confines of place and space. Yet within this theological maturation that asserts God's reign and sovereignty for all generations may reside a deepening disquiet. Given such absolute authority, why has God not responded to their suffering? If God does reign over all, what role has God played in bringing about this excess of suffering? No longer the national deity affiliated with Zion, would this omnipotent God even take notice of this people? The uneasiness residing in their theological affirmation of God's sovereignty and enduring reign erupts in the two questions that follow. "Why have you forgotten us completely? Why have you forsaken us these many days?" (5:20).

The fact that God resides apart from the destroyed temple should dispel their doubt. Instead, it evokes two inquiries that convey their accusation of what God has failed to do. God has "forgotten." God has "forsaken." The scope of God's non-attention is total (5:20a). This turning away by God is lengthy, as it spans "these many days" (5:20b). God's lack of response, perceived by the people as abandonment, is utterly comprehensive. Hence, their theology does not comfort them but may actually confound them and deepen their suffering. Their doubt and desperation echo in their inquiry and shed light on their deepest questions. Why has God not responded? Why has God not rescued us? Why has God punished us beyond that which is just?

As if without options, and despite the questions God's nonresponse raises, the people entreat the Lord (5:21). According to the literal Hebrew translation, here they ask God "to return" (שׁוב) to them so they will "be returned" (שׁוב) (5:21). This verb, שׁוב, is frequently enlisted to narrate the about-face or turning back that is required when one changes the course of life or turns away from an iniquitous path. Implied in this language is the people's willingness to be converted in their ways as well as a request that God make this possible. In addition, their desire to be returned to God con-

¹⁹But you, O Lᴏʀᴅ, reign forever;
your throne endures to all
generations.
²⁰Why have you forgotten us
completely?
Why have you forsaken us
these many days?

²¹Restore us to yourself, O Lᴏʀᴅ,
that we may be restored;
renew our days as of old—
²²unless you have utterly rejected
us,
and are angry with us beyond
measure.

veys their longing to be restored to a covenantal relationship. One might hear a faint tone of optimism embedded in their plea for restoration (5:21), but even the slightest temptation to hope must be vetted in conjunction with another realization. While everything depends on God's initiative and response, up until now there has been no divine response whatsoever.

A Theology That Confuses and Frightens

The theological confusion that characterizes deep human suffering is not difficult to grasp. Desperate, these survivors are asking God to restore them after asserting that this same God has utterly forgotten and forsaken them. They reproach the Lord for what has occurred while at the same time making a penitent overture to God to rescue them. The darkness and confusion that become the habitat of those suffering raise the question of the nature and existence of God in the most acute way. Thus, while the verse that follows and closes the poem is often thought to be at odds with this request "to return" and "to be returned," it is utterly congruent with the despondency after attempts to grasp God's role amid the suffering. Verse 19 recognizes the grandeur and sovereignty of God, while verse 20 accuses God of forsaking and forgetting the people. Verse 21 resorts to asking this same God to restore and reclaim them, as in the days of old, and then verse 22 closes with a consideration of whether God might ultimately reject them forever. The ambivalence and wavering across these final four verses characterize the dynamism of human suffering that engages in desperate overtures to behold God.

How to translate the opening of the final verse (5:22), כי אם־, has been the source of much conjecture.[8] Linafelt offers a persuasive translation

8. NRSV translates "unless" but the Hebrew accommodates an "if . . . then" syntactical construction, which will be followed here.

congruent with the content and longing of these poems. He reads the entire verse starting with כי אם־ as the "if" clause of the "if-then" syntactical construction, such that the last verse remains unfinished: "For if you have utterly rejected us, and are angry with us beyond measure. . . ."[9] No "then" clause follows that would complete the if-then construction. Thus, Linafelt concludes that "the book is left opening out into the emptiness of God's nonresponse."[10]

The community's final cry (5:22) seems to bespeak a dwindling faith in the midst of their suffering. Such a conclusion is difficult for those who hope for resolution by the end of this book. But Lamentations does not tell a linear story with a clear plot and resolution. The poems of this book are the testimonies of those in the midst of captivity and the grave elaboration of their famine, loss, torture, and humiliation. Any easy resolution would scoff at the survivor's reality and deny the hopelessness they face. It would insult the gut-wrenching outcries made audible in the five previous poems.

As a sanctuary for human sorrow, Lamentations does not offer a solution for the suffering it portrays even in this final chapter. Instead, this biblical book occasions a space where the disquiet associated with pain and sorrow can be expressed. Rather than offering easy explanations for human tragedy, it accommodates and features expressions of perplexity and confusion. It allows for the boldest theological musings about God in the midst of such suffering. It provides a space that can receive even blasphemous assertions. In this poetic chamber, pained voices make audible their theological questions and even reject religious notions of the past. They are allowed to resist denying the experience of suffering in the interest of defending any notions of theological orthodoxy. Lamentations offers a refuge for those riddled with doubt, darkness, desperation, and a sense of abandonment. It provides a haven for honest confession about the experience of suffering and the inner struggle that is, regrettably, often without resolution.

---

9. Here I am using the NRSV translation with the syntactical suggestion found in Tod Linafelt, *Surviving Lamentations: Catastrophe, Lament, and Protest in the Afterlife of a Biblical Book* (Chicago: University of Chicago Press, 2000), 60.
   10. Ibid.

Spending Holy Week with Lamentations

I decided to spend Holy Week reading and reflecting on Lamentations. I'd read somewhere that Christians often use this text during Lent, and I needed a focus for the week leading to Easter. I'd also read that the book probably recounts the destruction of the temple and the fall of Jerusalem, but I didn't get far before "here and now" intruded. The language on the page conjured up images from last night's newscast: once thriving cities in Syria bombed into ruins, children starving, mothers weeping, fathers staring into the distance as European countries close their borders. These images and the soundtrack of Lamentations merged in my mind and stopped me cold. Ancient words and timeless horrors. I think of the line from Ecclesiastes: "There is nothing new under the sun." —Day 1

* * *

"There are no words," I catch myself saying when I try to describe an experience of human suffering. When I hear myself fall back on that phrase, I wince. I am a writer. I made my living stringing words together, but now I often claim that I don't have the vocabulary to do justice to a particular moment of horror or grief or even love. I wonder, have I grown lazy? Has my vocabulary begun to wither and die? Or, at least in the cases of destruction, despair, and death that dominate television news,

am I simply defeated before I attempt the task?

Reading Lamentations I discover poetry that inventories destruction, sorts and freezes pain, peels back dignity, strips away humanity. The writer in me is brought to silence. —Day 2

* * *

What to make of the acrostic patterns of these five poems of Lamentations? It is a discipline for the writer to assume, a challenge to convey the collapse of a city and the lives it holds and to do so within the limits of a twenty-two-letter alphabet and still make sense. This couldn't have been an idle exercise, a trick to prove a vast vocabulary and unlimited imagination. Why this pattern? Scholars think that it may have been an effort to impose order *on* chaos. Or order *in* chaos. Or order *to* chaos. Whatever preposition we employ, the underlying notion makes sense to me. Especially when I realize there are, within the world of Lamentations and in our own, two constants: order and chaos. —Day 3

* * *

In the midst of Lamentations, there is hope. It makes a fleeting appearance in the middle verses of chapter 3, "For the LORD will not reject forever" (3:31). But the bulk of Lamentations stands in opposition. God does not seem to hear, acknowledge, or respond to the people's cries of despair. I think of Jesus praying in the Garden of Gethsemane, sending his own lament to a silent God,

"Let this cup pass from me"
(Matt 26:39). What do we make
of God's silence, especially when
we suffer, through our own fault,
or even, sometimes, innocently?
Are we redeemed through
suffering? Always? Sometimes?
I'm not sure. —Day 4

* * *

I find hope in Lamentations
4:1. Jerusalem's gold has grown
dim. "The sacred stones lie
scattered at the head of every
street." This line leaps out at me
and lures me back throughout
this week of reading. Why does
it seem hopeful to me?

Within the world of
Lamentations, destruction is total.
The temple is torn apart. Young
men and women lie dead in the
street. Elders sit in sackcloth and
dust. Prophets are all but blind.
Mothers contemplate eating
their children. But, in the midst
of the waste and wreckage,
"sacred stones" endure. The
city is destroyed; its people are
barely alive. But the stones used
to build their temple, the jewels
that adorned their faith, are not
ground to dust. They lie, not just
in some streets, but *at the head of
every street*."

Maybe these stones mark a way
forward. Remnants of a ruined
temple, they may still be sacred if
they inspire us to move, even one
step at a time, forward. That may
be all there is of hope in a world
where war decimates countries,
cities, neighborhoods, homes.
If we want to rebuild, there is
material to work with. —Day 5

* * *

Lamentations looks for a
witness: to the destruction
of Jerusalem and her people.
Daughter Zion calls out for God
to be that witness: to see the
consequences of what may be
divine judgment, to respond
with divine mercy and comfort.
But God is silent.

In reading Lamentations, I
become a witness. I reflect on
suffering, in the ancient world
and in my own. I relive the fear
and grief of my private losses
and remember that I am not
alone in suffering. I recognize
the apparent silence of God,
even as I refuse to read too
much into it. On a good day, my
wider faith reminds me that God
hears, witnesses, and eventually
redeems. It happened after the
fall of Jerusalem, after Jesus'
lonely prayer in Gethsemane.
It still happens. Perhaps more
often than I realize. —Day 6

* * *

Spending a week with
Lamentations reminds me that
sorrow and despair are part
of life. That a skillful writer
can impose order on chaos.
That elements of hope, though
broken and scattered, may
lie at the top of every street.
That laments may meet with
silence, but that silence may not
be final. And finally, that the
brutal and beautiful poetry of
Lamentations proves beyond
a doubt that there really *are*
words, after all. —Day 7

Nancy Haught

Conclusion

Lamenting Lamentations

L amentations transports the heartbreak and anguish of those who survived the destruction of Jerusalem and its subsequent siege in 587 BCE. With vivid description, these poems recount the pain and suffering of Zion's people in such a compelling way that for a reader not to be moved is virtually impossible. Yet there is more to lament here than the fate of Jerusalem's survivors who must confront the devastation and death surrounding them. In the course of narrating the demise of a nation, Lamentations casts a harrowing shadow over women. Most notable, Lamentations enlists the metaphor of Woman Zion as mother to evoke shame, pity, blame, and guilt.

The poems in Lamentations trace their form to ancient neighboring Mesopotamian city laments. Like the Mesopotamian compositions, these five laments portray their primary subject as a destroyed city responsible for its suffering inhabitants.[1] In the laments of these Mesopotamian neighbors, an associated goddess is the dominant speaking subject who pleads on behalf of the survivors. Many have identified Woman Zion of Lamentations as the counterpart to the goddess of these Mesopotamian

---

1. F. W. Dobbs-Allsopp, *Weep, O Daughter of Zion: A Study of the City-Lament Genre in the Hebrew Bible*, BibOr 44 (Rome: Pontifical Biblical Institute, 1993), 11–15.

laments.[2] Like Woman Zion, the goddess is often portrayed as a mother figure. The Mesopotamian figure is also a weeping goddess who cries out to her deity (Enlil) and others on behalf of her people.[3] Yet, despite the similarities in genre and portrayal of the key speaking figures in these laments, a significant difference in Israelite culture develops that distinguishes Woman Zion from the Mesopotamian goddess. The poems of Lamentations appear to collapse the destroyed city and the lamenting goddess into one metaphoric figure—a weeping widow who is then made responsible for her own catastrophe. Moreover, the development of her role across the five chapters serves to comprehensively indict her, gradually deny her speech, and eventually obscure her presence. The cultural evolution of a pleading mother goddess in the ancient Mesopotamian laments into a guilt-ridden widow depersonalized as "a filthy thing" (Lam 1:17d) in Israel's poems arouses legitimate suspicion and a question. Is there another loss here to lament besides the destruction of the city and its inhabitants? A tracing of the systematic disappearance of Woman Zion across these five chapters will not only disclose her degradation but also qualify her and all she represents as subject for our tears.

Lamentations 1 opens with a striking equity. Two speakers, a male observer and Woman Zion, each offer their perspective on the destruction of the city. Despite the differences in their perspectives, the quantity of airtime afforded each is remarkably balanced. Neither is privileged in terms of opportunity to recite. Additionally, both speakers interrupt each other only once. The observer delivers an apparently objective account that makes the destroyed city he describes a weeping mother whom later he blames for the catastrophe. Hence, he, the observer, speaks about the second speaker, Woman Zion. While to whom he offers his report is not clear, he notes bystanders and others who might be seeing what he sees. His description is dispassionate, though ultimately condemning. He notes that her friends have become her enemies, that her children have gone away, and that she is utterly alone. He narrates how her urban environment stands desolate. His narrative stems from observation and yet at

---

2. Ibid., 77; Tikva Frymer-Kensky, *In the Wake of the Goddesses: Women, Culture, and the Biblical Transformation of Pagan Myth* (New York: Ballantine Books, 1993), 170; and W. C. Gwaltney, "The Biblical Book of Lamentations in the Context of Near Eastern Lament Literature," in *Scripture in Context II: More Essays on the Comparative Method*, ed. W. W. Hallo, J. C. Moyer, and L. G. Perdue (Winona Lake, IN: Eisenbrauns, 1983), 208–9.

3. Dobbs-Allsopp, *Weep*, 78–87.

times reports rather intimate details of her experience. The enemies who have penetrated her narrow straits have stretched out their hands over her precious things. Her nakedness is made public, and she displays uncleanness in her skirts. In the course of his descriptions, the observer makes sense out of these horrific unfoldings by twice tying the catastrophe to the sinfulness of Woman Zion herself. Though never specifying the nature of this alleged sinfulness, he defines the terror and desolation afflicting this city woman as punishment for the "multitude of her transgressions" (1:5). When Woman Zion first speaks, she interrupts the observer, but she does not address her remarks to him. Rather, she speaks directly to God. In fact, she is the first to address God in Lamentations. As if to follow her lead, the next time the observer continues his oration, he too turns his remarks to the Lord. The chapter ends with Woman Zion's speech, in which she offers her own subjective experience of the calamity. What she describes is deeply personal and utterly compelling.

So persuasive is Woman Zion's account that when Lamentations 2 begins the observer's disposition has changed. He now becomes her advocate, empathizing with her and lashing out at the deity. Even though he holds God responsible for her suffering, he ultimately focuses on his own experience of affliction, which he features throughout his address. Curiously, the balanced speech allotments characteristic of Lamentations 1 disappear in this second poem. In this chapter, the observer's speech dominates, perhaps to compensate for the compromise in his perspective and relationship to Woman Zion. Since he now empathizes with her and defends her, he also presumes to speak for her.

The once Mesopotamian mother goddess, he now describes as Woman Zion—a city woman who has been dismantled and decimated beyond repair. Her children, the inhabitants, lay dying in the streets. Her ramparts, walls, and gates lay in ruins. Without qualification, the observer acknowledges that God's unbridled wrath instigated this destruction. Zion has borne the brunt of an assault by an out-of-control deity. Still, at the end of the poem he calls on Woman Zion, whom he has portrayed as a victim, to speak to her abuser. He summons her to call on God and seek reconciliation on behalf of the survivors, including himself. With this last occasion to make her voice heard, Woman Zion speaks. But she does not follow his instructions as to what she will say, nor does she assume the disposition he encourages. Instead, she delivers an unprecedented stinging oration to the deity that designates the god of retributive theology the real enemy. Like one recovering from violence who knows she must face her abuser, she confronts the deity with the carnage that has rendered her both as woman victim and as guilty woman. After such a show of boldness and such a glaring affront to the patriarchal mind-set, is there any reason to wonder why she is never heard from again for the remainder of the book?

As if to counter the strength that Woman Zion musters to face the one who has afflicted her and to match her strong affront to the male deity, Lamentations 3 opens with the account of a "strong man." His lament has been featured again and again as the centerpiece of the book because of the fleeting message of hope he forwards, but this hope is not founded on truth-telling. Furthermore, this hope dissipates by the end of the poem. This thin hope rests on old theology that requires denial of one's experience. It is an oration that lacks the strength of conviction of Woman Zion's final speech (2:20-22). The so-called strong man delivers a message weakened by his vacillations between confessing that he and the people have rebelled and then accusing God that they have not been forgiven. Moreover, his wavering between reporting his immense suffering and then denying the truth of his experience enfeebles any claims of strength tied to his identity. That Woman Zion, who rises from her broken status as victim to become a strong and resilient truth-teller in the preceding chapter, now disappears in this poem occasions no surprise. Her challenge to both the deity and to the patriarchal culture embedded with such a theology is unassailable.

Lamentations 4 continues the silence surrounding Woman Zion, offering no evidence of her whereabouts or of the impact of her speech until the very end of this poem. Instead, real women replace Woman Zion as victims. They are cited for their incapacity to rescue their dying infants and children during the long, drawn-out siege. Mothers are compared to ostriches to illustrate these women's failure to attend to their children's need for nourishment. Even jackals are cited as more caring of their offspring than Jerusalem's mothers. Unanswered cries of starving children and shriveled-up infants with tongues stuck to the roofs of their mouths imply women's lost capacity to respond. Yet, nowhere does the brokenness of women themselves, who are unable to provide for their babies, yield a lament. Only mothers' dried-up breasts and their inability to cause others to flourish receive detailed description. Nowhere do the cries of these heartbroken women, who still cradle their dying infants, command attention in these poems. Only the deplorable circumstances of children lying in the streets litter these verses. Finally, the level of moral depravity prompted by the prolonged enemy occupation enlists again an image debasing of women. As if to fulfill the Deuteronomic curse (Deut

28:53-57) for infidelity to covenant, the horrific conditions of the siege report that children are boiled and eaten by their mothers. The same suspicion and questions surrounding the fate of Woman Zion should be cultivated in regard to these mothers. How is it that this repugnant curse in Deuteronomy narrating fathers and mothers eating their children materializes in this account to tell of only mothers partaking in this cannibalism? How is it that in patriarchal culture the hierarchy of men—kings, military officers, priests, cultic officials—claims power for the administration of the community but is never assigned responsibility for its fate? How is it that the sign of this community's infidelity to the Lord rests at the feet of women? As metaphor fuses with and defines culture, the gradual but systematic degradation of Woman Zion now merges with and defines the diminishing status of the women of that community.

At the close of this fourth chapter, Woman Zion makes her final appearance in the whole of Lamentations. Yet she is not granted speech but serves only as object of a dubious description. The literal translation of the Hebrew reads, "Your punishment is complete, O daughter Zion" (4:22a). But because עֲוֺן can translate as either punishment for sin or as sin itself, "there is a question here about precisely what is complete."[4] Has Woman Zion's sinfulness finally come to an end? Or is this a statement that her punishment has finally finished? Even if the verse intends to assure that her punishment is complete, the consequences of her punishment linger as voiced by the community in the closing chapter, but this final description of Daughter Zion intends a contrast with Daughter Edom introduced in the preceding verse. Because sinfulness and shame of nakedness will become the fate of Daughter Edom, the contrast would also suggest that it is Woman Zion's sinfulness that is complete. Hence, in this final appearance, Woman Zion is left suspended between an end to her alleged sinfulness and an end to its punishment. Indefinite and obscured in this final appearance, she is rendered silent on the way to her complete erasure.

Only the collective voice of the suffering community cries out in the fifth and final poem of Lamentations. Again, the victimization of women figures in their prayerful testimony. Women are taken by enemy troops as war booty. This well-attested wartime hostility designed to insult men needs little elaboration as to the implied sexual assault and trauma that

---

4. Miriam Bier, *'Perhaps There Is Hope': Reading Lamentations as a Polyphony of Pain, Penitence, and Protest*, LHBOTS (New York: Bloomsbury T&T Clark, 2015), 161.

these women endured. But again, no lament goes up on behalf of these violated female members by their community. Moreover, no mention of Woman Zion falls from their lips. No memory of her tears and grief over the children she lost is recalled. No charge or indictment of her so-called sinfulness finds expression in the community's recitation. She is gone, utterly absent. Any remnant of an ancient Mesopotamian goddess that gave way to the metaphor of Woman Zion in the Israelite tradition has completely disappeared. Instead, Woman Zion, the metaphoric mother on whom iniquity was laid, became merged with the city. As the city met destruction, she herself was destroyed. Thus, in this final lament, she is lost in the recall of the community. Her individual voice and cries have been subsumed into the communal voice in this final lament. The boundaries between the metaphorical and the literal, and those between the individual and the communal, collapse. The erasure and silencing of Woman Zion appears complete.

The caution advised women in the opening of this commentary seems warranted. But even with caution, in what spirit can women even approach this book? On what terms can it function as Sacred Scripture for women believers? At first glance, Lamentations appears only to offer women a glimpse of the pain and suffering of Woman Zion and women during the exile. It may even aggravate wounds stemming from experiences of degradation or violence that a woman reader must bear.

Lamentations need not be read only as a narrative documenting the violence against women, however. Its proclamation may also be a means of both spiritual and political agency. When a community of women comes together and recites these laments, the spirit of Woman Zion emancipates from her silence. In communion with women's recitations, she, with them, testifies to her abuse and pain. She echoes in the voices of this community of women the indictments with which she has been charged as well as the suffering of her children she has borne. In addition, however, such recitations become an occasion for women themselves who have been victimized or abused to join their voices with Woman Zion, with other women in the community, and with their foremothers. For this poetic work can serve as more than evidence of women's mistreatment; it can also function as an invitation for the community of women down through the ages to name their pain and their suffering. It can emancipate women from the isolation, shame, and numbness caused by abuse. It can provide words for that kind of painful experience—whether divorce, a child's death, or domestic violence—that is sometimes thought to be utterly unspeakable. Within a community of women lamenters, recitations of these poems can provide the determination to overcome feelings of guilt, responsibility, and remorse that too often plague women victims. Bringing human suffering into view and lamenting it out loud provides agency to victims. In making public their pain and their anguish, women defeat denial. In giving voice to their experience, women refuse to preserve the silence that licenses victimizers to strike again. Hence, when women come together and pray these laments, their prayer becomes an act of protest. Women brought low by verbal degradation, the violence of war, or workplace injustices name their experience and, in the process of lamenting with a chorus of others, begin to rise again with self-respect and self-confidence.

Though Woman Zion is afflicted with pain and blame across these five poems, neither her cries nor the indictments against her have the last word. In a brief but nevertheless unprecedented recitation, Woman Zion lifts up her voice one final time in a powerful prayer (Lam 2:20-22) that in this interpretation becomes the focal point of the book. Abandoning self-blame, she assumes a resistant stance to the theological tradition that has indicted her. Instead, she demands the divine take note of her suffering. Then she lets loose an angry tirade at the god of a bankrupt theological tradition through which she and other women have been scapegoated. The warrior deity who abuses, violently punishes, and makes innocent children victims bears no resemblance to the ancient goddess weeping for her children. Such a tyrannical force conceived as a deity is at best the concoction and reflection of the competitive dynamism inherent in an oppressive hierarchical order. Named patriarchy, this subjugating order produces a theology reflective of itself. A patriarchal deity must wield unbridled power at the top to maintain its position and, in the process, destroys community by stratifying social classes below.

Hence, when Woman Zion confronts the deity, she also challenges this theology. Audaciously, she names this deity "the enemy." She gives voice not only to her own emancipation from the clutches of self-blame and victimhood; she also occasions a prayer space for other women to express their anger and their pain. And in the process, women can move forward in an embrace of the full value of their lives as women and begin to recognize the real Holy Presence within their midst.

Works Cited

Bakhtin, Mikhail. M. *Problems of Dostoevsky's Poetics*. Edited and translated by Caryl Emerson. Minneapolis: University of Minnesota Press, 1984.

Bartlett, John R. *Edom and the Edomites*. JSOTSup 77. Sheffield: Sheffield Academic, 1989.

Bergant, Dianne. *Lamentations*. AOTC. Nashville: Abingdon, 2003.

Berges, Ulrich. "The Violence of God in the Book of Lamentations." In *One Text, a Thousand Methods: Studies in Memory of Sjef Van Tilborg*, edited by Patrick Chatelion Counet and Ulrich Berges, 21–44. Boston: Brill, 2005.

Berlin, Adele. *Lamentations*. Louisville: Westminster John Knox, 2002.

Bier, Miriam J. *'Perhaps There Is Hope': Reading Lamentations as a Polyphony of Pain, Penitence, and Protest*. LHBOTS. New York: Bloomsbury T&T Clark, 2015.

Boase, Elizabeth. *The Fulfilment of Doom?: The Dialogic Interaction between the Book of Lamentations and the Pre-Exilic/Early Exilic Prophetic Literature*. LHBOTS 437. New York: T&T Clark, 2006.

Boda, Mark J., Carol Dempsey, and LeAnn Snow Flesher, eds. *Daughter Zion: Her Portrait, Her Response*. Atlanta: SBL Press, 2012.

Brown, Francis, S. R. Driver, Edward Robinson, Charles A. Briggs, and Wilhelm Gesenius. *A Hebrew and English Lexicon of the Old Testament: With an Appendix Containing the Biblical Aramaic*. Oxford: Clarendon, 1979.

Brown, Paula, and Donald F. Tuzin, eds. *The Ethnography of Cannibalism*. Washington, DC: Society for Psychological Anthropology, 1983.

Childs, Brevard S. *Introduction to the Old Testament as Scripture*. Philadelphia: Fortress, 1979.

Dobbs-Allsopp, F. W. *Lamentations*. IBC. Louisville: John Knox, 2002.

———. *Weep, O Daughter of Zion: A Study of the City-Lament Genre in the Hebrew Bible*. BibOr 44. Rome: Pontifical Biblical Institute, 1993.

Dobbs-Allsopp, F. W., and Tod Linafelt. "The Rape of Zion in Thr 1,10." *ZAW* 113 (2001): 77–81.

Frymer-Kensky, Tikva. *In the Wake of the Goddesses: Women, Culture, and the Biblical Transformation of Pagan Myth*. New York: Ballentine Books, 1993.

Garrett, Duane A., and Paul R. House. *Song of Songs/Lamentations*. WBC 23B. Nashville: Nelson, 2004.

Gottwald, Norman K. *Studies in the Book of Lamentations*. Chicago: A. R. Allenson, 1954.

Guest, Deryn. "Hiding Behind the Naked Women in Lamentations: A Recriminative Response." *BibInt* 7 (1999): 413–48.

Gwaltney, W. C. "The Biblical Book of Lamentations in the Context of Near Eastern Lament Literature." In *Scripture in Context II: More Essays on the Comparative Method*, edited by W. W. Hallo, J. C. Moyer, and L. G. Perdue, 191–211. Winona Lake, IN: Eisenbrauns, 1983.

Hens-Piazza, Gina. "Forms of Violence and the Violence of Forms: Two Cannibal Mothers before a King (2 Kings 6:24-33)." *JFSR* 14 (1998): 91–104.

———. "Learning to Curse: Catharsis, Confession, and Communion in the Psalms." *Review for Religious* 53 (Winter 1994): 860–65.

———. *Nameless, Blameless and without Shame: Two Cannibal Mothers before a King*. Interfaces. Collegeville, MN: Liturgical Press, 2003.

Hillers, Delbert R. *Lamentations*. AB 7A. Garden City, NY: Doubleday, 1992.

Lakoff, G., and M. Turner. *More Than Cool Reason: A Field Guide to Poetic Metaphor*. Chicago: University of Chicago Press, 1989.

Landy, Francis. "Lamentations." In *The Literary Guide to the Bible*, edited by Robert Alter and Frank Kermode. Cambridge, MA: Belknap Press, 1987.

Lee, Archie Chi Chung. "Mothers Bewailing: Reading Lamentations." In *Her Master's Tools? Feminist and Postcolonial Engagements of Historical-Critical Discourse*, edited by Caroline Vander Stichele and Todd C. Penner, 195–210. GPBS 9. Atlanta: SBL Press, 2005.

Linafelt, Tod. *Surviving Lamentations: Catastrophe, Lament, and Protest in the Afterlife of a Biblical Book*. Chicago: University of Chicago Press, 2000.

Longman, Tremper, III. *Jeremiah, Lamentations*. NIBC. Peabody, MA: Hendrickson, 2008.

Mandolfo, Carleen R. *Daughter Zion Talks Back to the Prophets: A Dialogic Theology of the Book of Lamentations*. SemeiaSt 58. Atlanta: SBL Press, 2007.

McDaniel, Thomas. "Philological Studies in Lamentations." *Bib* 49 (1968): 27–53.

Miller, Charles William. "Reading Voices: Personification, Dialogism, and the Reader of Lamentations 1." *BibInt* 9 (2001): 393–408.

Mintz, Alan. *Hurban: Responses to Catastrophe in Hebrew Literature*. New York: Columbia University Press, 1984.

Newsom, Carol A. *The Book of Job: A Contest of Moral Imaginations*. Oxford: Oxford University Press, 2003.

————. "A Maker of Metaphors: Ezekiel's Oracles against Tyre." In *Interpreting the Prophets*, edited by J. L. Mays and P. J. Achtemeier, 188–99. Philadelphia: Fortress, 1987.

O'Connor, Kathleen M. "Lamentations." In *Women's Bible Commentary*, edited by Carol A. Newsom, Sharon H. Ringe, and Jacqueline E. Lapsley, 280–85. 3rd ed. Louisville: Westminster John Knox, 2012.

————. *Lamentations and the Tears of the World*. Maryknoll, NY: Orbis Books, 2002.

Parry, Robin A. *Lamentations*. THOTC. Grand Rapids: Eerdmans, 2010.

Provan, Iain. *Lamentations*. New Century Bible Commentary. Grand Rapids: Eerdmans, 1991.

Pyper, Hugh S. "Reading Lamentations." *JSOT* 95 (2001): 55–69.

Renkema, Johan. *Lamentations*. Translated by Brian Doyle. HCOT. Leuven: Peeters, 1998.

Ryken, Philip Graham. *Jeremiah and Lamentations: From Sorrow to Hope*. Preaching the Word. Wheaton, IL: Crossway, 2001.

Salters, Robert B. *Lamentations: A Critical and Exegetical Commentary*. ICC. New York: T&T Clark, 1994.

Sanday, Peggy Reeves. *Divine Hunger: Cannibalism as a Cultural System*. Cambridge: Cambridge University Press, 1986.

Seidman, Naomi. "Burning the Book of Lamentations." In *Out of the Garden: Women Writers on the Bible*, edited by C. Buchmann and C. Spiegel, 278–88. New York: Fawcett Columbine, 1992.

Shlain, Leonard. *The Alphabet Versus the Goddess: The Conflict between Word and Image*. New York: Penguin Press, 1999.

Tigay, Jeffrey Howard, Alan Cooper, and Bathja Bayer. "Lamentations, Book of." In *Encyclopedia Judaica*, edited by Fred Skolnik and Michael Berenbaum, 2nd ed., vol. 12, 446–51. Detroit: Macmillan, 2007.

Trible, Phyllis. *God and the Rhetoric of Sexuality*. OBT. Philadelphia: Fortress, 1978.

Weems, Renita. *Battered Love: Marriage, Sex, and Violence in the Hebrew Prophets*. Minneapolis: Fortress, 1995.

Westermann, Claus. *Lamentations: Issues and Interpretation*. Translated by Charles Muenchow. Minneapolis: Fortress, 1994.

Wright, Christopher. *The Message of Lamentations*. Downers Grove, IL: InterVarsity Press, 2015.

Index of Scripture References

9:11	9

Nehemiah

9:17	65
31	65

Job

19:9	86

Psalms

2	67
9	45, 67
14	67
20	67
23	41
36:5	45
40:11	45
44	77
46:3	67
48	67
48:1-3	67
50	45, 67
60	77
74	77
75:9	72
78:38	65
79	77
80	77
86:15	65
88:12	45
89:2-3	45
89:13	23
92:3	45
98:3	45
100:5	45
103:8	65
111:4	65
132	67
135	67
137:7	71

145:8	65

Isaiah

10	45
22	72
27:13	79
34:5-17	71
41:10	23
47:1-3	10
47:3	8
51:17	72
54:8	45
63:1-6	71
63:7	45

Jeremiah

3:12	45
9:17-20	xlviii
9:23	45
10:11	xxxv n. 45
16:5	45
17	72
25:15	71, 72
25:16	72
28	72
31:3	45
31:29-31	81
32:18	45
33:11	45
39:1-10	xxxix
51:7	72

Ezekiel

4:1-17	xxxix
16:36-37	8
18	8
18:1-4	81
23:10	8
23:31-33	72
25:12-14	71

32:16-18	xlviii
35:3-15	71

Daniel

2:4–7:28	xxxv n. 45

Hosea

2:21	45
9:3	79
11:5	79

Joel

2:13	65
4:19	71

Obadiah

1:1-18	71

Jonah

4:2	65

Micah

7:18	45

Nahum

3:5	8

Habakkuk

2:16	72

Zechariah

7:9	45
10:10-11	79

Malachi

1:2-5	71

1 Corinthians

7:9	xxiii

Index of Subjects

General Editor

Barbara E. Reid, OP, is a Dominican Sister of Grand Rapids, Michigan. She holds a PhD in biblical studies from The Catholic University of America and is vice president and academic dean and professor of New Testament studies at Catholic Theological Union, Chicago. Her most recent publications are *Wisdom's Feast: An Invitation to Feminist Interpretation of the Scriptures* (2016) and *Abiding Word: Sunday Reflections on Year A, B, C* (3 vols.; 2011, 2012, 2013). She served as president of the Catholic Biblical Association in 2014–2015.

Volume Editor

Carol J. Dempsey, OP, PhD, is professor of theology (biblical studies) at the University of Portland, Oregon. Her primary research interest is in prophetic literature as it relates to the ancient and contemporary world. Her recent publications include *The Bible and Literature* (Orbis Books, 2015) and *Amos, Hosea, Micah, Nahum, Habakkuk, and Zephaniah: A Commentary* (Liturgical Press, 2013) and numerous articles related to prophets, gender studies, ethics, and environmental concerns. She is a member of the Dominican Order of Caldwell, New Jersey.

Author

Gina Hens-Piazza is Joseph S. Alemany Professor of Biblical Studies at the Jesuit School of Theology of Santa Clara University, a school within the Graduate Theological Union in Berkeley, California. She is a frequent lecturer nationally and internationally. Hens-Piazza received her PhD and MPhil from Union Theological Seminary, New York, and her MA from Vanderbilt University.